FICTION
TO 14

CHRISTOPHER EDGE

OXFORD
UNIVERSITY PRESS

OXFORD
UNIVERSITY PRESS

Great Clarendon Street, Oxford, OX2 6DP, United Kingdom

Oxford University Press is a department of the University of Oxford.
It furthers the University's objective of excellence in research, scholarship,
and education by publishing worldwide. Oxford is a registered trade mark
of Oxford University Press in the UK and in certain other countries

© Oxford University Press 2017

The moral rights of the author have been asserted

First published in 2017

British Library Cataloguing in Publication Data

Data available

ISBN 978-019-837685-9

10 9 8 7 6 5 4 3 2 1

MIX
Paper from
responsible sources
FSC® C007785

Printed in Great Britain by Bell and Bain Ltd., Glasgow

Acknowledgements

The author and publisher are grateful for the permission to reprint extracts
from the following copyright material:

Isabel Allende: *The City of Beasts* translated by Margaret Sayers Peden
(Fourth Estate, 2013), copyright © Isabel Allende 2002, English translation
copyright © HarperCollins Publishers Inc, 2002, reprinted by permission of
HarperCollins Publishers Ltd.

Malorie Blackman: *Chasing the Stars* (Doubleday, 2016), copyright ©
Malorie Blackman 2016, reprinted by permission of The Random House
Group Ltd.

Ray Bradbury: 'The Night', copyright © Ray Bradbury 1946, from *Dark
Carnival* (Hamish Hamilton, 1948), reprinted by permission of Abner Stein/
Don Congdon Associates for the Estate of Ray Bradbury.

Susan Cooper: *The Dark is Rising* (Chatto & Windus, 1973), copyright © Susan
Cooper 1973, reprinted by permission of The Random House Group Ltd.

Gillian Cross: *After Tomorrow* (OUP, 2013), copyright © Gillian Cross 2013,
reprinted by permission of Oxford University Press.

Roald Dahl: 'A Piece of Cake' from *The Wonderful World of Henry Sugar and Six
More* (Puffin, 2013), copyright © Roald Dahl 1977, reprinted by permission
of David Higham Associates.

Anita Desai: 'Games at Twilight' from *Games at Twilight: and Other Stories*
(Vintage, 1998), copyright © Anita Desai 1978, reprinted by permission of
Rogers Coleridge & White Ltd, 20 Powis Mews, London, W11 1JN.

Siobhan Dowd: *The London Eye Mystery* (David Fickling, 2007), copyright ©
Siobhan Dowd 2007 reprinted by permission of The Random House Group Ltd.

Daphne Du Maurier: *Rebecca* (Virago, 2012), copyright © Daphne Du
Maurier 1938, reprinted by permission of Curtis Brown Group Ltd, London
on behalf of The Beneficiaries of the Estate of Daphne d Du Maurier.

Nathan Filer: *The Shock of the Fall* (HarperCollins, 2013), copyright © Nathan
Filer 2013, reprinted by permission of HarperCollins Publishers Ltd.

Esther Freud: *Hideous Kinky* (Penguin, 1993), copyright © Esther Freud
1992, reprinted by permission of Penguin Books Ltd.

William Goldman: *The Princess Bride* (Bloomsbury, 1999), copyright © William
Goldman 1973, reprinted by permission of Bloomsbury Publishing Plc.

Graham Greene: *Brighton Rock* (Vintage Classics, 2011), copyright ©
Graham Greene 1938, reprinted by permission of David Higham Associates.

Frances Hardinge: *The Lie Tree* (Macmillan, 2015), copyright © Frances
Hardinge 2015, reprinted by permission of Macmillan Children's Books, an
imprint of Pan Macmillan, a division of Macmillan Publishers International Ltd.

Susan Hill: *The Woman in Black* (Vintage, 2015), copyright © Susan Hill 1983,
reprinted by permission of Sheil Land Associates Ltd.

Kazuo Ishiguro: *Never Let Me Go* (Faber, 2005), copyright © Kazuo Ishiguro
2005, reprinted by permission of Faber & Faber Ltd.

Franz Kafka: *Metamorphosis* translated by David Wyllie (Ebooks @ Adelaide,
2004), English translation copyright © David Wyllie 2002, reprinted by
permission of David Wyllie.

Stephen Kelman: *Pigeon English* (Bloomsbury, 2011), copyright © Stephen
Kelman 2011, reprinted by permission of Bloomsbury Publishing Plc.

Andrea Levy: *Small Island* (Headline, 2005), copyright © Andrea Levy 2004,
reprinted by permission of Headline Publishing Group Ltd.

C S Lewis: letter from *Letters to Children* edited by Lyle W Dorsett and
Marjorie Lamp Mead (Touchstone, 1995), copyright © C S Lewis Pte Ltd
1985, reprinted by permission of The C S Lewis Company Ltd..

Louis Nowra: *Into that Forest* (Egmont, 2012), copyright © Amanita Pty
Ltd 2012, reprinted by permission of Egmont UK Ltd and Allen & Unwin,
Australia (www.allenandunwin.com)

Emmuska Orczy Baroness Orczy: 'The Woman in the Big Hat' from
Lady Molly of Scotland Yard (Cassell, 1910), reprinted by permission of United
Agents LLP on behalf of Sarah Orczy-Barstow Brown.

R J Palacio: *Wonder* (Doubleday, 2012), copyright © R J Palacio 2012,
reprinted by permission of The Random House Group Ltd.

Philip Reeve: *Railhead* (OUP, 2015), copyright © Philip Reeve 2015,
reprinted by permission of Oxford University Press.

Muriel Spark: *The Pride of Miss Jean Brodie* (Penguin, 2000), copyright ©
Muriel Spark 1961, reprinted by permission of David Higham Associates.

Meera Syal: *Anita and Me* (HarperCollins, 2006) copyright © Meera Syal
1997, reprinted by permission of HarperCollins Publishers Ltd.

John Wyndham: *The Day of the Triffids* (Penguin, 1951), copyright © John
Wyndham 1951, reprinted by permission of David Higham Associates.

Although we have made every effort to trace and contact all copyright
holders before publication this has not been possible in all cases. If notified,
the publisher will rectify any errors or omissions at the earliest opportunity.

The author and publisher would like to thank the following for their
permission to use their photographs:

Cover: Vera Holera/Shutterstock, YAY Media AS/Alamy Stock Vector;
p13: Dover Books/Public Domain/OUP; **p28:** Railhead, Philip Reeve, 2015/
Reproduced by permission of Switch Press; **p38:** AF archive/Alamy Stock
Photo; **p40:** Entertainment Pictures/Alamy Stock Photo; **p49:** sjbooks/
Alamy Stock Photo; **p53:** annaav/123rf; **p54-55:** arcticphotoworks/123RF;
p57: Paweł Opaska/123rf; **p59:** Steffan Hill/Alamy Stock Photo; **p62:** Everett
Collection Inc/Alamy Stock Photo; **p65:** AF archive/Alamy Stock Photo;
p73: Chronicle/Alamy Stock Photo; **p76:** World History Archive/Alamy
Stock Photo; **p82:** MAC1/Shutterstock; **p87:** © Martinmates/Dreamstime;
p88: AF Fotografie/Alamy Stock Photo; **p95, 97:** AF archive/Alamy Stock
Photo; **p100:** Photo 12/Alamy Stock Photo; **p103:** iStockphoto; **p106:**
Small Island, Angela Levy, 2004/Reproduced by permission of St Martin's
Press; **p113:** Daniel Nicolae/123rf; **p115:** AF archive/Alamy Stock Photo;
p117: Entertainment Pictures/Alamy Stock Photo; **p119, 123:** iStockphoto;
p124: Pigeon English, Stephen Kelman, 2011/Reproduced by permission of
Bloomsbury Publishing; **p127:** Pictorial Press Ltd/Alamy Stock Photo; **p129:**
Everett Collection Inc/Alamy Stock Photo; **p131:** AF archive/Alamy Stock
Photo; **p135:** Mark Garlick/Alamy Stock Photo; **p140:** Pagina/Shutterstock;
All other photos © Shutterstock.

Every effort has been made to contact copyright holders of material
reproduced in this book. Any omissions will be rectified in subsequent
printings if notice is given to the publisher

Introduction

Welcome to *Fiction to 14*, a brand new book in this bestselling series which has proven hugely popular with students and teachers all around the world.

Fiction is a way of understanding the world. Through the stories we read, we can walk in other people's shoes, experience different ways of life, and visit strange and unfamiliar places. In this book we have brought together extracts from novels and short stories from the 19th, 20th and 21st centuries, organizing these in ways that will help students to explore different aspects of fiction, from the creation of character, setting and voice, to establishing genre, structure and theme.

These high-quality texts have been chosen to stimulate, engage and challenge students, building their understanding of the author's craft and developing their appreciation of literature from around the world. The accompanying activities are designed to develop the skills students need to read and respond to fiction, from comprehension skills to analysing how language and structure can be used to convey meaning and create deliberate effects.

As well as developing students' skills as critical readers of fiction, specific activities in *Fiction to 14* are also designed to nurture students' skills as writers of fiction, enabling them to draw on the techniques they have explored in their reading when writing themselves. Additional activities are also designed to help students make comparisons across and between texts, further developing their critical reading skills.

As an author, I know that fiction can open the door to many amazing worlds. I hope you find that *Fiction to 14* can guide you on your own adventures in the world of fiction.

Christopher Edge

Contents

How to use this book

Structure

The structure of *Fiction to 14* is straightforward, with each chapter focusing on a key aspect of fiction, as detailed on the contents pages. Each chapter is designed to support students as they develop their reading and writing skills, with the level of challenge increasing as students work through the chapter, as well as increasing progressively through the book as a whole.

Big picture

Each chapter begins with a 'Big picture' section to introduce the aspect of fiction that the chapter will explore. This 'Big picture' links the aspect of fiction to students' own reading experiences, and asks a 'big question' to help students contextualize the texts they are about to explore.

Skills

Fiction to 14 has been designed to develop a range of reading and writing skills:

- Understand the meaning of a text
- Make inferences and refer to evidence in a text
- Comment on a writer's use of language
- Comment on a writer's use of structure
- Understand how setting, plot, voice and characterization are created
- Compare texts
- Practise writing fiction, drawing on techniques explored in reading

These skills move from the more literal requirements of reading – that is, comprehension – to the higher-level skills of critical reading involved in studying fiction, including comparing texts and exploring how setting, plot, voice and characterization are created and conveyed. In addition to this, students will develop their skills in writing fiction, drawing on the techniques explored in their reading.

Before reading

This section provides activities that enable students to locate the texts they will read in context. By encouraging students to draw links with their own wider reading, and making links with other forms of entertainment, the 'Before reading' activities will activate students' prior knowledge of the aspect of fiction in focus and help them to begin to consider the key features they explore in the texts they will read.

Source texts

Each chapter includes three extracts from fiction, including novels and short stories. These include extracts from children's, young adult and adult fiction, from a range of noted authors from around the world, including literary greats, award-winning writers, and even a Children's Laureate. Of the three extracts included in each unit, one text is from the 19th Century, one is from the 20th Century, and one text is from the 21st Century. These high-quality extracts have been chosen to illustrate the aspect of fiction in focus, but the aim too is to engage students as readers and encourage them to seek out the novels and short stories the extracts are taken from, to broaden their wider reading.

Each text is preceded by a short introduction, designed to help students quickly understand the source of the text and the context for the extract they are about to read. In this introduction, students will also be asked a question to help them to engage more actively with the text that follows. This question can be set as a reading task, but many are also designed for discussion because high-quality talk feeds high-quality reading and writing.

Basic and advanced reading questions

The questions that follow each text are divided into 'basic' and 'advanced' reading questions. The basic questions generally demand decoding and comprehension. The advanced questions require students to explore language and structural features, making judgements about how different aspects of fiction such as voice, characterization, setting and theme are established and conveyed, and the effects created by these.

Extended reading and writing activities

Each chapter ends with two extended assignments: an extended reading activity and an extended writing activity. These extended activities are designed to develop the skills explored in greater detail, sometimes asking students to orchestrate a range of skills in their responses.

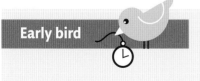

Early bird

The 'Early bird' feature at the end of each chapter is designed to provide students who complete their reading and writing activities with a quirky challenge to keep them engaged. These 'Early bird' activities include word games, writing challenges and puzzles, and aim to reward students who have completed a task in a motivating way.

Exploring language and structural features

When you read and respond to a fiction text, you might be asked to explore a writer's use of language or structure. Look at the tables below to remind yourself of some of the features of language and structure you could look out for. Remember that as well as identifying these different features in a text, you need to be able to explain the effects they create.

Exploring language Look at the table below to remind yourself of some of the most common grammatical features used at word and phrase level.

Grammatical feature	Definition	Example
Noun	A word used to name a person, place or thing	The *pen* is mightier than the *sword*. The *danger* is *overconfidence*.
Adjective	A word which describes a noun	It was a *jagged* cliff. The weather grew *cold*.
Verb	A word that identifies actions, thoughts, feelings or the state of being	I *believe* this is true. She *shouts* at me to *stop*. *Leave* him alone.
Tense	The tense of the verb tells you when the action of the verb takes place (present, past or future)	I *am washing* the car now. I *washed* the car yesterday. I *will wash* the car tomorrow.
Adverb	A word that adds meaning to a verb, adjective or another adverb	It was *strangely* quiet. *Sometimes* we have pizza for tea. We looked *everywhere*.
Adverbial	A group of words that function as an adverb	He worked *very hard*. The dog slept *under the table*.

Now look at the table below to remind yourself of some of the most common literary techniques.

Literary technique	Definition	Example
Alliteration	The repetition of the same letter or sound at the beginning of a group of words for special effect	Drab and depressing
Dialogue	Words spoken by characters in a play, film or story	'I can't work it out, can you?' 'No, this kind of device was never my strong point,' Jake replied.
Emotive language	Words and phrases that arouse emotion	This wasn't death; this was murder.
Hyperbole	A deliberately exaggerated statement that is not meant to be taken literally	He was the size of an elephant.
Imagery/descriptive detail	Writing which creates a picture or appeals to other senses – this includes simile, metaphor and personification and the use of vivid verbs, nouns, adjectives and adverbs	We knew the house smelt fusty and dank but we didn't expect the lacy cobwebs and the oozing walls.
Metaphor	The use of a word or phrase which describes something by likening it to something else	He was a monkey in class.
Onomatopoeia	Words which imitate the sound they represent	Buzz, pop, crackle
Pathetic fallacy	A literary technique where a character's emotions are reflected or represented by the environment or landscape	The storm raged outside as she wept by the fire.
Personification	A form of metaphor whereby an inanimate object is given the qualities of a living being	The rocks reached for the sky.
Repetition	Words or phrases which are repeated for effect	She ran, ran for her life.
Sibilance	The use of the 's' sound at the beginning or within neighbouring words	The geese seemed to whisper and snigger as he sidled past.
Simile	A comparison where one thing is compared to another using the words *like* or *as*	He was as quiet as a mouse.
Tricolon (pattern of three)	Groups of three related words or phrases placed close together	The paint was peeling, the windows were cracked and the floorboards were rotting.

Exploring structural features

Structural features can include the sentence forms a writer uses, for example, the sentence types (that is, statement, question, command, exclamation) and sentence structures (that is, single and multi-clause sentences) used.

Look at the table below to remind yourself of some of the most common structural features at sentence level.

Structural feature	Explanation	Example
Clause	Part of a sentence with its own verb	After she ran down the road
Simple sentence (single clause sentence)	The most basic type of sentence consisting of a subject and a verb	The girl stood.
Compound sentence (a type of multi-clause sentence)	A sentence containing two independent clauses linked by a coordinating conjunction	The dog ate his dinner but I had nothing.
Complex sentence (a type of multi-clause sentence)	A sentence containing a main clause and one or more subordinate clauses linked by a subordinating conjunction such as *because, as, although* or a relative pronoun such as *who, that* or *which*.	The boy, who lived next door to me, was older than I was.

When you look at the structure of a text, you should also explore the following aspects:

- the sequence through a text, that is, how the text is organized
- the focus through a text, that is, where the writer is directing the reader's attention
- the coherence of a text, that is, the connections made between ideas, themes, and so on.

The questions in the table below can help you to explore these aspects of structure in the texts you read.

Aspect of structure	Questions to ask yourself
Sequence	■ Is the narrative told in chronological order or does it include flashback or non-chronological content? ■ How are characters, setting and events introduced? ■ Is there a pivotal moment or climax which the author leads up to? ■ Are any elements of action, gesture, dialogue or description repeated within the text? ■ Can you spot any patterns?
Focus	■ What narrative viewpoint is the story told from (that is, first person, second person, third person)? ■ How is the narrative spotlight placed on particular characters, events, places or feelings? ■ What is the balance between dialogue, action and description? ■ Can you identify any contrasts or opposites within the text? ■ Are there shifts in mood, setting or perspectives?
Coherence	■ Are different parts of the text (such as the opening and ending) connected in any way? ■ Can you identify any links within or across paragraphs? ■ Are any paragraphs particularly long or short or used to create a specific effect?

Source texts table

Texts	Date
1.1 'The Woman in the Big Hat' by Baroness Orczy	1910
1.2 *Chasing the Stars* by Malorie Blackman	2016
1.3 'Lost Hearts' by M. R. James	1895

Big picture

When you walk into a bookshop, you will find adult fiction from different **genres** on different shelves and in different sections. From crime and horror to science-fiction and romance, every type of story can usually be categorized as belonging to a certain genre. What kind of stories do you like to read and watch? In this section you'll read extracts from a novel and short stories from the 19th, 20th and 21st centuries, and explore the genres their authors are writing in.

Skills

- Understand the meaning of a text

- Make inferences and refer to evidence in the text

- Explore the features of different genres of fiction

- Study how setting, plot and characterization are established

- Practise writing fiction in different genres, drawing on techniques explored in reading

Key term

genre a particular style or type of story

Before reading

1 Can you think of at least one story for each genre listed below? This might be a favourite story or maybe one you have just heard about.

science-fiction romance mystery thriller
fantasy comedy spy historical
crime horror adventure

2 Choose your favourite genre from the above list and explain why you like this type of story. Try to support your explanation with examples from novels and stories you have read.

1.1 'The Woman in the Big Hat' by Baroness Orczy, 1910

The following extract is taken from the short story 'The Woman in the Big Hat' by Baroness Orczy, which was first published in 1910. Set in the early part of the 20th century, 'The Woman in the Big Hat' features a female police detective named Lady Molly of Scotland Yard. Here, Lady Molly and her assistant Mary Granard arrive at a London cafe to discover that a customer has been found dead. As you read, think about which genre the story belongs to.

Source text 1.1

WORD BANK

paraphernalia various pieces of equipment or belongings

awry twisted to one side

particulars details or facts

Here two of our men were busy with pencil and notebook, whilst one fair-haired waitress, dissolved in tears, was apparently giving them a great deal of irrelevant and confused information.

Chief Inspector Saunders had, I understood, been already sent for; the constables, confronted with this extraordinary tragedy, were casting anxious glances towards the main entrance, whilst putting the conventional questions to the young waitress.

And in the alcove itself, raised from the floor of the room by a couple of carpeted steps, the cause of all this commotion, all this anxiety, and all these tears, sat huddled up on a chair, with arms lying straight across the marble-topped table, on which the usual **paraphernalia** of afternoon tea still lay scattered about. The upper part of the body, limp, backboneless, and **awry**, half propped up against the wall, half falling back upon the outstretched arms, told quite plainly its weird tale of death.

Before my dear lady and I had time to ask any questions, Saunders arrived in a taxicab. He was accompanied by the medical officer, Dr Townson, who at once busied himself with the dead man, whilst Saunders went up quickly to Lady Molly.

'The chief suggested sending for you,' he said quickly; 'he was phoning you when I left. There's a woman in this case, and we shall rely on you a good deal.'

'What has happened?' asked my dear lady, whose fine eyes were glowing with excitement at the mere suggestion of work.

'I have only a few stray **particulars**,' replied Saunders, 'but the chief witness is that yellow-haired girl over there. We'll find out what we can from her directly Dr Townson has given us his opinion.'

The medical officer, who had been kneeling beside the dead man, now rose and turned to Saunders. His face was very grave.

WORD BANK

morphia morphine, a drug made from opium

beverage drink

muff a short tube-shaped piece of warm material into which the hands are pushed from opposite ends

'The whole matter is simple enough, so far as I am concerned,' he said. 'The man has been killed by a terrific dose of **morphia** – administered, no doubt, in this cup of chocolate,' he added, pointing to a cup in which there still lingered the cold dregs of the thick **beverage**.

'But when did this occur?' asked Saunders, turning to the waitress.

'I can't say,' she replied, speaking with obvious nervousness. 'The gentleman came in very early with a lady, somewhere about four. They made straight for this alcove. The place was just beginning to fill, and the music had begun.'

'And where is the lady now?'

'She went off almost directly. She had ordered tea for herself and a cup of chocolate for the gentleman, also muffins and cakes. About five minutes afterwards, as I went past their table, I heard her say to him, "I am afraid I must go now, or Jay's will be closed, but I'll be back in less than half an hour. You'll wait for me, won't you?"'

'Did the gentleman seem all right then?'

'Oh, yes,' said the waitress. 'He had just begun to sip his chocolate, and merely said "S'long" as she gathered up her gloves and **muff** and then went out of the shop.'

'And she has not returned since?'

'No.'

'When did you first notice there was anything wrong with this gentleman?' asked Lady Molly.

'Well,' said the girl with some hesitation, 'I looked at him once or twice as I went up and down, for he certainly seemed to have fallen all of a heap. Of course, I thought that he had gone to sleep, and I spoke to the manageress about him, but she thought that I ought to leave him alone for a bit. Then we got very busy, and I paid no more attention to him, until about six o'clock, when most afternoon tea customers had gone, and we were beginning to get the tables ready for dinners. Then I certainly did think there was something wrong with the man. I called to the manageress, and we sent for the police.'

Basic reading skills

1   Re-read the opening paragraph.

   a   List two facts about the waitress.

   b   List one opinion the narrator gives about the waitress.

2   What reason does Chief Inspector Saunders give for wanting Lady Molly's help with this case?

3   What does Dr Townson say is the cause of the man's death?

4a Re-read the extract and note down any key facts or clues that you think might help to solve the case.

4b Who do you think is responsible for the man's death? Give reasons for your answer, referring to evidence from the text.

Advanced reading skills

1 Copy and complete the following table. Identify the features of the crime genre that can be found in the extract.

Features of the crime genre	Evidence from the extract
A serious crime	A man is found dead at his table in a cafe, 'killed by a terrific dose of morphia'
A detective or investigator	
Suspects	
Villain	
Clues	

2 The narrator comments that 'The upper part of the body... told quite plainly its weird tale of death.' Re-read this sentence and explain what it means in your own words.

3a The story is narrated by Lady Molly's assistant Mary Granard; Lady Molly herself does not figure significantly in this extract. Why do you think the writer has made this decision?

3b What impression do you get of Lady Molly? In your answer you should comment on:

- how the narrator describes Lady Molly
- how other characters act towards Lady Molly
- what Lady Molly says and does in the extract.

4 This story was first published in 1910. How does the writer's use of language indicate when the story was written? In your answer, you should comment on:

- the writer's choice of vocabulary
- the use of different **sentence forms**
- the **formality** of the language.

Refer to evidence from the text to support the points you make.

5 Choose the statement below that you most agree with and complete it in your own words.

> I think this extract is an effective example of crime fiction because...

> I think this extract is a poor example of crime fiction because...

Key terms

sentence forms
sentence types (that is, statement, question, command, exclamation) and sentence structures (that is, single and multi-clause sentences)

formality how formal or informal the language used is as indicated by vocabulary choice, sentence forms, use of Standard English and so on

1.2 *Chasing the Stars* by Malorie Blackman, 2016

The following extract is taken from the novel *Chasing the Stars* by Malorie Blackman. Here, Nathan is escaping from an alien species called the Mazon, but the spaceship he is travelling on has come under attack. As you read, think about which genre the story belongs to.

Source text 1.2

WORD BANK

DE blast directed-energy blast

A strange, strangled hush had descended on the cargo hold. Darren was kneeling on the ground, with his head in his hands, grief making his whole body quake. The ship we were on was still rising, juddering and jolting as we moved through the planet's atmosphere, leaving our friends and loved ones behind. I looked around, shaking my head. There were so few of us left. At first glance I'd say around twenty-odd. Would we get the chance to rescue the others before the Mazon wiped them out? Without warning, the ship shook violently, knocking those few still standing off their feet. That last blast had been too close. If just one **DE blast** were to hit us, then we'd be toast.

Mum came and sat down next to me. She put her arm around my shoulder and kissed my forehead. I let it pass as it might be the last kiss I got from her. We were on an Earth vessel. That meant we weren't out of danger, far from it. A cocktail of emotions stirred within me. Back on the planet surface, I really thought my last moments had come. Now here I was in the cargo hold of some anonymous Earth ship. Some of my friends were back down on the planet surface, no doubt still having to endure the continuing Mazon attack. I could only hope they'd make it to the cavern in the mountains. But was I any safer on this ship which could be blasted out of the sky at any moment?

Every second counted and was precious because it could be my last. I made a vow in that moment never to squander a single second of my life again. If by another miracle we got out of this alive, I would grab hold of life and squeeze every drop out of it.

A strange mist descended from the vents above us. I knew a moment's foreboding at the sight of it but if someone wished us harm, they'd hardly go to the trouble of rescuing us first. However, this was an Authority Earth Vessel. Had we really come this far only to be recaptured? The thought made me feel physically sick. I would fight and die before I let them take me back.

'Mum, d'you recognize this ship?' I whispered.

Mum shook her head.

I looked around again. What kind of captain was in charge of this vessel? Would he or she listen to the truth about us and at least give us a chance? Or had we jumped out of the frying pan and straight into the fire?

Basic reading skills

1 Re-read the opening paragraph.

    a In what part of the spaceship is the extract set?

    b How many people does Nathan say he can see on board?

    c Pick out a quotation that shows the effect of the blast as the spaceship comes under attack.

2 Why do you think Nathan's mother kisses Nathan?

3 What emotions do you think Nathan is feeling in this extract? Choose three emotions from the list below and justify your choices with reference to the text.

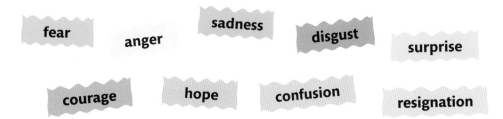

fear   anger   sadness   disgust   surprise

courage   hope   confusion   resignation

4 If he survives Nathan says, 'I would grab hold of life and squeeze every drop out of it.' Using your own words, explain what he means by this.

5 What do you predict might happen next in the story?

Advanced reading skills

1 What impression do you get of Nathan? Explore how the following help to build this impression:

- Nathan's thoughts and what these suggest about his character
- Nathan's dialogue and how he acts towards his mother
- Nathan's reactions to the events of the scene.

2 Re-read the opening paragraph. How does the way this paragraph is structured help to build a sense of tension? Think about:

- what the writer focuses your attention on at the start of the paragraph
- the sequence of events described in the paragraph and how Nathan reacts to these
- the sentence forms used and the effects these create
- what the writer focuses your attention on at the end of the paragraph.

3 How does the writer's use of language help to build tension throughout the extract? In your answer you should comment on the effects created by:

- the writer's choices of vocabulary and descriptive details
- the writer's choices of **verbs**, **adverbs** and **adjectives**
- the writer's use of questions and other sentence forms.

4 Read what the following student has written about this text:

Although it uses the ingredients of science fiction, it feels like a very human story.

Explain what you think this student means and then say whether you agree or disagree with the statement. Give reasons for your answer.

Key terms

verb a word that identifies actions, thoughts, feelings or the state of being

adverb a word that adds to the meaning of a verb, adjective or another adverb

adjective a word that describes a noun

1.3 'Lost Hearts' by M.R. James, 1895

The following extract is taken from the short story 'Lost Hearts' by M. R. James, which was first published in 1895. In this story a young boy called Stephen Abney has been invited by his older cousin Mr Abney to stay at his home, Aswarby Hall. Here, Stephen is looking out of his bedroom window at night as he waits to meet his uncle in his study at 11pm. As you read, think about which genre the story belongs to.

Source text 1.3

WORD BANK

mere lake

The wind had fallen, and there was a still night and a full moon. At about ten o'clock Stephen was standing at the open window of his bedroom, looking out over the country. Still as the night was, the mysterious population of the distant moonlit woods was not yet lulled to rest.

From time to time strange cries as of lost and despairing wanderers sounded from across the **mere**. They might be the notes of owls or water-birds, yet they did not quite resemble either sound.

Were not they coming nearer? Now they sounded from the nearer side of the water, and in a few moments they seemed to be floating about among the shrubberies.

Then they ceased; but just as Stephen was thinking of shutting the window and resuming his reading of *Robinson Crusoe*, he caught sight of two figures standing on the gravelled terrace that ran along the garden side of the Hall — the figures of a boy and girl, as it seemed. They stood side by side, looking up at the windows.

Something in the form of the girl recalled irresistibly his dream of the figure in the bath. The boy inspired him with more acute fear.

Whilst the girl stood still, half-smiling, with her hands clasped over her heart, the boy, a thin shape, with black hair and ragged clothing, raised his arms in the air with an appearance of menace and of unappeasable hunger and longing.

The moon shone upon his almost transparent hands, and Stephen saw that the nails were fearfully long and that the light shone through them.

As he stood with his arms thus raised, he disclosed a terrifying spectacle. On the left side of his chest there opened a black and gaping rent; and there fell upon Stephen's brain, rather than upon his ear, the impression of one of those hungry and desolate cries that he had heard resounding over the woods of Aswarby all that evening.

WORD BANK

effect bring about
(make it happen)

In another moment this dreadful pair had moved swiftly and noiselessly over the dry gravel, and he saw them no more.

Inexpressibly frightened as he was, he determined to take his candle and go down to Mr. Abney's study, for the hour appointed for their meeting was near at hand.

The study or library opened out of the front hall on one side, and Stephen, urged on by his terrors, did not take long in getting there.

To **effect** an entrance was not so easy. The door was not locked, he felt sure, for the key was on the outside of the door as usual. His repeated knocks produced no answer. Mr. Abney was engaged: he was speaking. What! Why did he try to cry out? And why was the cry choked in his throat? Had he, too, seen the mysterious children?

But now everything was quiet, and the door yielded to Stephen's terrified and frantic pushing.

Basic reading skills

1a What sounds does Stephen hear from across the mere?

1b What two creatures does the narrator suggest might be responsible for these sounds?

2 What does Stephen see outside his window?

3 Find a phrase or sentence that suggests that Stephen is more frightened by the figure of the boy than the girl. Explain your choice.

4a Re-read the paragraph beginning 'Whilst the girl stood still...' Choose a word from the list below that best describes the atmosphere created in this paragraph.

tense   fearful   claustrophobic   calm

sinister

4b Select the quotation that you think most effectively contributes to creating this atmosphere. Give reasons for your choice.

5 Re-read the second to last paragraph. What does Stephen hear inside Mr Abney's room?

Advanced reading skills

1 What impression does the writer create of the figures of the boy and girl? In your answer you should comment on the way language is used to convey:

- their appearances
- their actions
- Stephen's reactions to them.

2 Explain what genre you think this extract belongs to. Pick out textual details to support your explanation and give reasons for your choice.

3 Look again at the extract from 'Inexpressibly frightened as he was...' Explain what the different sentence forms and types used in these paragraphs suggest about Stephen's thoughts and feelings at this point in the story. Think about the effects created by:

- the use of multi-clause sentences
- the use of a simple sentence
- the use of questions.

4 How does the writer create a sense of Stephen's mounting fear? Think about how both language and structure are used to build tension and convey Stephen's growing panic.

Extended reading

Look back at the three extracts you have read in this section. Which extract do you think is the best example of the genre it belongs to? Use some or all of these questions to structure your response.

- What happens in the text and how does it fit your expectations of this genre of story?

- Do you think the setting reflects a typical setting found in this genre of story?

- In what ways does the main character in the extract reflect the **protagonist** you would expect to find in this genre of story?

- Did the extract make you want to read the rest of the story? Why or why not?

Extended writing

Choose one of the extracts you have read in this section. Write the next part of the story. Think about how you can maintain the writing style and genre of your chosen extract. In your writing you should:

- continue the narrative with a scene that follows directly on from the extract you have read

- maintain the **narrative voice** established in the extract

- use description, action and dialogue to maintain or change the mood of the scene

- use language and structure to create deliberate effects that are appropriate to the genre you are writing in.

Remember to check the spelling, punctuation and grammar of your writing.

Key terms
protagonist the main character
narrative voice the voice that tells the story; for example, in the first-person narrative of *Chasing the Stars* this voice belongs to Nathan, while in the other two extracts the narrative voice is an authorial voice. See the sections on Viewpoint (pages 46–57) and Voice (pages 58–67) for more information.

Early bird

Make up your own titles for the following genres of story, for example, *The Fangs of Doom* for a horror story.

crime   horror   science-fiction   romance   thriller

adventure   fantasy   comedy   mystery   spy   historical

Source texts table

Text	Date
2.1 'Games at Twilight' by Anita Desai	1978
2.2 *Railhead* by Philip Reeve	2015
2.3 *Dracula* by Bram Stoker	1897

Big picture

When you start reading a story you enter a world that the author has created. This might be a place that you recognize such as a cluttered garage or an everyday town. Or you might discover an unfamiliar invented world such as J. R. R. Tolkien's Middle-earth or Lewis Carroll's Wonderland. Which **settings** from stories you have read stick in your mind? In this section, you will read extracts from two novels and one short story and explore the techniques their authors use to help readers visualize the settings they create.

Skills

- Understand the meaning of a text
- Make inferences and refer to evidence in the text
- Comment on a writer's use of language, including imagery and **figurative language**, in creating an effective setting
- Compare texts
- Create engaging and evocative settings in your own stories

Before reading

Key terms

setting the time and place in which a story is set

figurative language language that uses words for the effects they create, rather than their literal meanings

1   Match the following fictional settings to the books they can be found in.

Narnia	*The Colour of Magic*
Panem	*The Amber Spyglass*
Ankh-Morpork	*The Hunger Games*
Hogwarts Castle	*Harry Potter and the Philosopher's Stone*
Prentisstown	*The Lion, the Witch and the Wardrobe*
Cittàgazze	*The Knife of Never Letting Go*

2   Think about a book that you have read that contained a memorable setting. Write a brief description of this setting and why you found this memorable.

2.1 'Games at Twilight' by Anita Desai, 1978

The following text is taken from 'Games at Twilight', a short story by Anita Desai about a young boy called Ravi who is playing a game of hide and seek with the other children in his family. Here, Ravi decides to hide in a shed as his older relative Raghu searches for him. As you read, try to visualize the setting of the story.

Source text 2.1

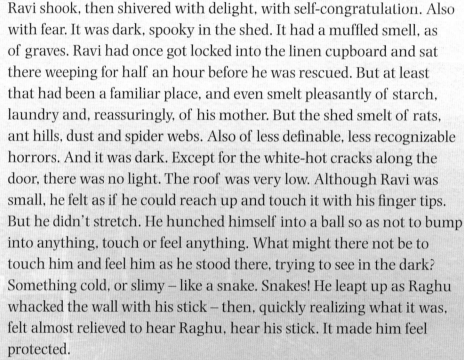

Ravi shook, then shivered with delight, with self-congratulation. Also with fear. It was dark, spooky in the shed. It had a muffled smell, as of graves. Ravi had once got locked into the linen cupboard and sat there weeping for half an hour before he was rescued. But at least that had been a familiar place, and even smelt pleasantly of starch, laundry and, reassuringly, of his mother. But the shed smelt of rats, ant hills, dust and spider webs. Also of less definable, less recognizable horrors. And it was dark. Except for the white-hot cracks along the door, there was no light. The roof was very low. Although Ravi was small, he felt as if he could reach up and touch it with his finger tips. But he didn't stretch. He hunched himself into a ball so as not to bump into anything, touch or feel anything. What might there not be to touch him and feel him as he stood there, trying to see in the dark? Something cold, or slimy – like a snake. Snakes! He leapt up as Raghu whacked the wall with his stick – then, quickly realizing what it was, felt almost relieved to hear Raghu, hear his stick. It made him feel protected.

But Raghu soon moved away. There wasn't a sound once his footsteps had gone around the garage and disappeared. Ravi stood frozen inside the shed. Then he shivered all over. Something had tickled the back of his neck. It took him a while to pick up the courage to lift his hand and explore. It was an insect – perhaps a spider – exploring *him*. He squashed it and wondered how many more creatures were watching him, waiting to reach out and touch him, the stranger.

There was nothing now. After standing in that position – his hand still on his neck, feeling the wet splodge of the squashed spider gradually dry – for minutes, hours, his legs began to tremble with the effort, the inaction. By now he could see enough in the dark to make out the large solid shapes of old wardrobes, broken buckets and bedsteads piled on top of each other around him. He recognized an old bathtub – patches of enamel glimmered at him and at last he lowered himself onto its edge.

Basic reading skills

1 Re-read the opening paragraph. What different emotions is Ravi feeling here?

2 List four things that the shed smells of.

3 What is the only source of light in the shed?

4 Explain why you think Ravi hunches himself into a ball.

5 Why does Ravi begin to tremble in the final paragraph?

6 Draw a simple sketch of the setting. Use labels and arrows to highlight any specific details.

Advanced reading skills

Key terms

repetition words or phrases which are repeated for effect

imagery writing which creates a picture or appeals to other senses – this includes simile, metaphor and personification and the use of vivid verbs, nouns, adjectives and adverbs

conjunction a word that usually joins words, phrases or clauses in a sentence, for example, *and, but, although*

1 Re-read the opening paragraph. What other location does the author contrast the current setting with? What effect does this create?

2 Look at the following descriptive details from the text. Choose one and explain how it conveys Ravi's fear.

    'It was dark, spooky in the shed.'

    'It had a muffled smell, as of graves.'

    'The roof was very low.'

3 Writers can use **repetition** for emphasis or to draw the reader's attention to specific details. Find an example of repetition in the extract and explain the specific effect it creates.

4a Writers can convey atmosphere through their choice of **imagery**. Choose an adjective from the list below that best describes the atmosphere of the text.

cheerful   **claustrophobic**

tense   **sinister**   **calm**

4b Select the quotation that you think most effectively contributes to creating this atmosphere. Give reasons for your choice.

5 How does the writer's use of sentence forms and punctuation help to build up a picture of the setting? You should comment on:

   ■ the use of **conjunctions** to start sentences

   ■ the effects created by the use of different types of punctuation such as commas and dashes

   ■ the length of different sentences and the effects they create.

6 At the end of the extract, do you think Ravi wants to be found? Refer to the text to support your answer.

2.2 *Railhead* by Philip Reeve, 2015

The following text is taken from *Railhead*, a novel by Philip Reeve, which describes a future where intelligent trains travel between the stars. Here, Zen, a young petty thief, is trying to escape from a drone that is following him and enters Ambersai station where the trains depart for other planets. As you read, try to visualize the setting.

Source text 2.2

WORD BANK

litanies long lists

rickshaw a two-wheeled carriage pulled by one or more people

touted tried to sell something or get business

disembarking getting off a vehicle

Ambersai station: grand and high-fronted like a great theatre, with the K-bahn logo hanging over its entrance in letters of blue fire. Booming loudspeaker voices reciting **litanies** of stations. Moths and Monk bugs swarming under the lamps outside; beggars and street kids too, and buskers, and vendors selling fruit and chai and noodles, and **rickshaw** captains squabbling as they **touted** for fares. Through the din and the chatter came the sound of the train.

Zen went through the entrance barriers and ran out onto the platform. The Express was just pulling in. First the huge loco, a Helden Hammerhead, its long hull sheathed in shining red-gold scales. Then a line of lit windows, and a pair of station angels flickering along the carriage sides like stray rainbows. Some tourists standing next to Zen pointed at them and snapped pictures which wouldn't come out. Zen kept his place in the scrum of other K-bahn travellers, itching to look behind him, but knowing that he mustn't because, if the drone was there, it would be watching for just that: a face turned back, a look of guilt.

The doors slid open. He shoved past **disembarking** passengers into a carriage. It smelled of something sweet, as if the train had come from some world where it was springtime. Zen found a window seat and sat there looking at his feet, at the ceramic floor, at the patterns on the worn seat coverings, anywhere but out of the window, which was where he most wanted to look. His fellow passengers were commuters and a few Motorik couriers with their android brains stuffed full of information for businesses further down the line. In the seats opposite Zen lounged a couple of rich kids: railheads from K'mbussi or Galaghast, pretty as threedie stars, dozing with their arms around each other. Zen thought about taking their bags with him when he got off, but his luck was glitchy tonight and he decided not to risk it.

The train began to move, so smoothly that he barely noticed. Then the lights of Ambersai Station were falling behind, the throb of the engines was rising, the backbeat of the wheels quickening. Zen risked a glance at the window. At first it was hard to make out anything in the confusion of carriage reflections and the city lights sliding by outside. Then he saw the drone again. It was keeping pace with the train, shards of light sliding from its rotor blades as it burred along at window height, aiming a whole spider-cluster of eyes and cameras and who-knew-what at him.

The train rushed into a tunnel, and he could see nothing any more except his own skinny reflection, wide cheekbones fluttering with the movement of the carriage, eyes big and empty as the eyes on moths' wings.

The train accelerated. The noise rising, rising, until, with a soundless bang—a kind of *un-bang*—it tore through the K-gate, and everything got reassuringly weird. For a timeless moment Zen was outside of the universe. There was a sense of falling, although there was no longer any down to fall to. Something that was not quite light blazed in through the blank windows...

Then another un-bang, and the train was sliding out of another ordinary tunnel, slowing towards another everyday station. It was bright daytime on this world, and the gravity was lower. Zen relaxed into his seat, grinning. He was imagining that drone turning away in defeat from the empty tunnel on Ambersai, a thousand light years away.

Basic reading skills

1 Re-read the opening paragraph.

   a List three details that show Ambersai station is a noisy place.

   b List four types of people who can be seen at the station.

2 How do Zen's actions indicate that he is nervous? List one detail from the text and explain how this suggests his nervousness.

3 Zen's luck is described as 'glitchy'. Write down what you think 'glitchy' means in this context.

4 What is Zen being followed by?

5 Re-read the closing paragraph. Write down two ways in which this world is different from the world Zen has just left.

Advanced reading skills

Key terms

simile a comparison where one thing is compared to another using the words *like* or *as*

metaphor the use of a word or phrase which describes something by likening it to something else

onomatopoeia words which imitate the sounds they represent

1 Figurative language, including **similes** and **metaphors**, is often used by authors to create comparisons that can help to convey settings and characters in vivid and interesting ways.

   a Ambersai station is described as 'grand and high-fronted like a great theatre'. What impression does this give you of the station?

   b Identify three more examples of figurative language from the text. Choose the example you think is most effective and explain the impression it creates.

2 Look at the description of the Express. Choose one adjective from the list below that best describes the impression the writer gives you of the train.

impressive   **majestic**   **grand**

shabby   **ordinary**

Select a textual detail that you think helps to create this impression and explain the reason for your choice.

3 The writer uses **onomatopoeia** to describe the movement of the drone 'as it burred along'. What does the verb 'burred' make you think of the way the drone is moving?

4a The writer describes the train travelling through the K-gate 'with a soundless bang—a kind of *un-bang*'. Explain how the writer plays with language here and what effect it creates.

4b Select two other details that help to convey the experience of travelling between the stars. Explain the effect each of these details helps to create.

5 Read what this student says about the text:

I think the writer takes a familiar experience and makes it extraordinary.

Explain what you think this student means and then say whether you agree or disagree with the statement. Give reasons for your answer.

2.3 *Dracula* by Bram Stoker, 1897

The following extract is taken from the novel *Dracula* by Bram Stoker. Jonathan Harker, a young solicitor from England, is being taken to Castle Dracula in Transylvania at night in a horse-drawn coach. As you read, notice how the author uses language to create a vivid setting.

Source text 2.3

Soon we were hemmed in with trees, which in places arched right over the roadway till we passed as through a tunnel; and again great frowning rocks guarded us boldly on either side. Though we were in shelter, we could hear the rising wind, for it moaned and whistled through the rocks, and the branches of the trees crashed together as we swept along. It grew colder and colder still, and fine, powdery snow began to fall, so that soon we and all around us were covered with a white blanket. The keen wind still carried the howling of the dogs, though this grew fainter as we went on our way. The baying of the wolves sounded nearer and nearer, as though they were closing round on us from every side. I grew dreadfully afraid, and the horses shared my fear; but the driver was not in the least disturbed. He kept turning his head to left and right, but I could not see anything through the darkness.

WORD BANK

illumine light up

beetling overhanging

import meaning

Suddenly, away on our left, I saw a faint flickering blue flame. The driver saw it at the same moment; he at once checked the horses, and, jumping to the ground, disappeared into the darkness. I did not know what to do, the less as the howling of the wolves grew closer; but while I wondered the driver suddenly appeared again, and without a word took his seat, and we resumed our journey. I think I must have fallen asleep and kept dreaming of the incident, for it seemed to be repeated endlessly, and now, looking back, it is like a sort of awful nightmare. Once the flame appeared so near the road that even in the darkness around us I could watch the driver's motions. He went rapidly to where the blue flame arose—it must have been very faint, for it did not seem to **illumine** the place around it at all—and gathering a few stones, formed them into some device. Once there appeared a strange optical effect: when he stood between me and the flame he did not obstruct it, for I could see its ghostly flicker all the same. This startled me, but as the effect was only momentary, I took it that my eyes deceived me straining through the darkness. Then for a time there were no blue flames, and we sped onwards through the gloom, with the howling of the wolves around us, as though they were following in a moving circle.

At last there came a time when the driver went further afield than he had yet done, and during his absence the horses began to tremble worse than ever and to snort and scream with fright. I could not see any cause for it, for the howling of the wolves had ceased altogether; but just then the moon, sailing through the black clouds, appeared behind the jagged crest of a **beetling**, pine-clad rock, and by its light I saw around us a ring of wolves, with white teeth and lolling red tongues, with long, sinewy limbs and shaggy hair. They were a hundred times more terrible in the grim silence which held them than even when they howled. For myself, I felt a sort of paralysis of fear. It is only when a man feels himself face to face with such horrors that he can understand their true **import**.

calèche a type of horse-drawn carriage

impalpable
 imperceptible

All at once the wolves began to howl as though the moonlight had had some peculiar effect on them. The horses jumped about and reared, and looked helplessly round with eyes that rolled in a way painful to see; but the living ring of terror encompassed them on every side, and they had perforce to remain within it. I called to the coachman to come, for it seemed to me that our only chance was to try to break out through the ring and to aid his approach. I shouted and beat the side of the **calèche**, hoping by the noise to scare the wolves from that side, so as to give him a chance of reaching the trap. How he came there, I know not, but I heard his voice raised in a tone of imperious command, and looking towards the sound, saw him stand in the roadway. As he swept his long arms, as though brushing aside some **impalpable** obstacle, the wolves fell back and back further still. Just then a heavy cloud passed across the face of the moon, so that we were again in darkness.

When I could see again the driver was climbing into the calèche, and the wolves had disappeared. This was all so strange and uncanny that a dreadful fear came upon me, and I was afraid to speak or move. The time seemed interminable as we swept on our way, now in almost complete darkness, for the rolling clouds obscured the moon. We kept on ascending, with occasional periods of quick descent, but in the main always ascending. Suddenly, I became conscious of the fact that the driver was in the act of pulling up the horses in the courtyard of a vast ruined castle, from whose tall black windows came no ray of light, and whose broken battlements showed a jagged line against the moonlit sky.

Basic reading skills

1 Re-read the opening paragraph. List three things you learn about the weather.

2 What makes the driver stop the coach?

3 The narrator reports seeing a strange optical effect. In your own words, explain what this is.

4a What causes the horses pulling the coach to 'snort and scream with fright'?

4b Find a phrase or sentence in the text which tells you that the narrator experiences the same emotion.

5 What causes the wolves to disappear?

6 Draw a map showing the narrator's journey to Castle Dracula as described in the text. Use labels and arrows to highlight any specific details about the landscape the coach travels through and the incidents that occur on the journey.

Advanced reading skills

1 Look again at the opening sentence: 'Soon we were hemmed in with trees, which in places arched right over the roadway till we passed as through a tunnel; and again great frowning rocks guarded us boldly on either side.'

a What impression does this sentence give you of the setting?

b How does the writer's use of **prepositions** help to create a claustrophobic sense of place?

2a Create a tension graph to plot how the tension builds in the text. Label the Y axis 'Scale of tension' and the X axis 'Key details and quotations'. You should record the details and quotations that help to create a tense or unsettling atmosphere on the graph, positioning these to show the rise and fall of tension in the text.

2b Identify the point in the text where you think the tension reaches a climax.

3 Look again at the final paragraph where the narrator arrives at Dracula's castle. What impression do you get of this location? How does the writer use language to convey this?

4 Read what this student says about the text:

I think the setting is quite **clichéd**.

Explain what you think the student means and say whether you agree or disagree with their statement. Justify your answer with references to the text.

Key terms

preposition a word used with a noun or pronoun to show place, position, time or means, for example, *over* the roadway

cliché an idea that is used so often that it has little meaning

Extended reading

Compare the extracts you have read from 'Games at Twilight' and *Dracula* in order to answer the following question.

Compare how the settings created by the two writers help to convey an atmosphere of fear. In your answer, you could:

■ compare the different settings (the similarities and differences)

■ compare the methods the writers use to create their settings

■ explore how these convey an atmosphere of fear

■ support your ideas with references to both texts.

Extended writing

Think about the place where you live and use this as the setting for the following scene.

> An intruder breaks into a property. This person is searching for something important that they believe is hidden there.

As you write, think about:

■ the viewpoint you are writing from – could this be in the first person from the viewpoint of the intruder or somebody in the house or in the third person using an authorial voice?

■ the atmosphere you want to create, such as a mood of fear, and how your description of the setting can help to convey this

■ how you can use vocabulary and figurative language to create deliberate effects

■ how you can weave details about the setting into the action.

Remember to check the spelling, punctuation and grammar of your writing.

Early bird

Can you describe a setting in a sentence? Use adjectives from the selection below to convey an impression of a setting in a sentence. How many different settings can you create?

arid   bare   barren   bleak   craggy   enclosed   exposed   fallow

farmed   fenced   fertile   furrowed   hilly   inhospitable   irrigated   jagged

lunar   lush   mountainous   open   patchwork   pitted   ploughed

rocky   rugged   shady   sheltered   steep   sun-drenched   wooded

Pick your favourite sentence and expand this into a paragraph that describes the setting in more detail.

Source texts table

Text	Date
3.1 *Anita and Me* by Meera Syal	1996
3.2 *A Christmas Carol* by Charles Dickens	1843
3.3 *The Lie Tree* by Frances Hardinge	2015

Big picture

Who is your favourite fictional character? From heroes like Harry Potter that get their name in the title of the book to unforgettable villains such as Long John Silver from *Treasure Island*, the plot of a story is driven by the actions of its characters. In this section you will read extracts from novels written in the 19th, 20th and 21st centuries and explore the techniques their authors use to create memorable characters.

Skills

- Make inferences and refer to evidence in the text
- Comment on a writer's use of language and structure to convey character
- Compare texts
- Use techniques explored in your reading to write a new scene for *A Christmas Carol*

Before reading

1   Think about a fictional character that you know well. This could be a favourite character from a short story, novel, film, television drama or video game. Copy and complete the following character profile to summarize what you remember about him or her.

   Character name:

   Distinguishing features:

   Habits/mannerisms:

   Strengths and qualities:

   Weaknesses and flaws:

   What the character wants – their key desire or goal in the story:

2   Look at the following statement by the author Janet Burroway:

   'A flat character is one who has only one distinctive characteristic... A round character is many faceted and is capable of change.'

   Discuss whether you think the character you have created the profile for is a flat character or a round character. Think about whether they only have one distinctive characteristic or a multifaceted personality. Give reasons for your choice.

3.1 *Anita and Me* by Meera Syal, 1996

The following text is taken from the novel *Anita and Me* by Meera Syal. Set in the 1970s the novel is about Meena Kumar, a nine-year-old girl growing up in the only Punjabi family in the village of Toddington, near Birmingham, and her relationship with her friend Anita. Here, Meena's parents have invited Anita to their house for dinner after learning that Anita's mother has left home. In the extract, Anita refers to Tracey, her sister, and Meena to Sunil, her younger brother. As you read, think about the impression you get of the different characters.

Source text 3.1

Anita turned up alone and empty-handed, wearing her new school jumper with a pair of flared jeans. 'Tracey didn't want to come,' was the first thing she said to my parents who stood by the door, as they did for all our visitors, ready to take her coat. 'Oh, that's okay, darling,' said mama, ushering her in and waving at papa to remove one of the place settings from the dining table. I had insisted that we sit at the table, something we never did with Indian guests since we usually ate in shifts. But tonight, I had set the table myself, even putting Sunil's high chair next to mama's place, and told her, 'Don't just run to and from the kitchen burning your fingers like you normally do. I want us to sit and talk, you know, like you're supposed to do at dinners.' I could have asked mama to tap-dance on top of the telly... playing the spoons and she might have considered it, so anxious was she to mop the brow of our motherless guest.

I knew Anita well enough not to expect a great display of mourning, but even I was surprised by her complete lack of emotion, or indeed, social graces. She watched *Top of the Pops* through all papa's attempts to engage her in friendly chit-chat, during which he steered clear of anything that might possibly be connected with Mothers. 'So Anita... um, how's school?' Anita grunted and turned up the volume control, shifting away from Sunil who was edging towards her holding the edge of the sofa, desperate to make friends with this new face. 'Your par... your father; does he take you or do you go by bus?' Anita stifled a yawn and reached for another crisp from our nick-nacks bowl, as mama called it, which was now almost empty.

Mama had gone to the trouble of preparing two menus, which was fortunate considering Anita's reaction when the serving dishes of various curries were placed in front of her. 'What's that!' she demanded, as if confronted with a festering sheep's head on a platter. 'Oh that's mattar-paneer,' mama said proudly, always happy to educate the sad English palate. 'A sort of Indian cheese, and these are peas with it, of course...'

'Cheese and peas?' said Anita faintly. 'Together?'

'Well,' mama went on hurriedly. 'This is chicken curry... You have had chicken before, haven't you?'

'What's that stuff round it?'

'Um, just gravy, you know, tomatoes, onions, garlic...' Mama was losing confidence now, she trailed off as she picked up Anita's increasing panic.

'Chicken with tomatoes? What's garlic?'

'Don't you worry!' papa interjected heartily, fearing a culinary cat fight was about to shatter his fragile peace. 'We've also got fishfingers and chips. Is tomato sauce too dangerous for you?'

Anita's relief made her oblivious to his attempt at a joke. She simply picked up her knife and fork and rested her elbows on the table, waiting to be served with something she could recognise. 'I'll have fishfingers, mum! Um, please!' I called out after her. I could tell from the set of mama's back that her charity was wearing a little thin. Although I had yet to cast Anita in the mould of one of the Rainbow orphan kids, I did wonder if food was a problem at her house after seeing her eat. Any romantic idea I had about witty stories over the dinner table disappeared when Anita made a fortress of her arms and chewed stolidly behind it, daring anyone to approach and disturb her concentration or risk losing an eye if they attempted to steal a chip. She looked up only twice, once when my parents began eating, as always, with their fingers, using their **chapatti** as scoops to ferry the banquet of curries into their mouths.

Anita stopped in mid-chew, looking from her knife and fork to mama and papa's fingers with faint disgust, apparently unaware that all of us had a great view of a lump of half **masticated** fishfinger sitting on her tongue.

WORD BANK

chapatti a flat cake of unleavened bread, used in Indian cookery

masticated chewed

Basic reading skills

1   Re-read the first paragraph.

  a   What does Anita wear to dinner?

  b   Who has set the table for dinner?

  c   How does Meena say her mother usually behaves during dinner and how does she want her to act?

2a   Meena says that she is surprised by Anita's lack of 'social graces'. In your own words, say what you think this means.

2b   Give one example of Anita's behaviour that you think best demonstrates her lack of social graces.

3   Meena's mother has prepared several dishes for dinner. What does she say 'mattar-paneer' is?

4   What does Meena say she wants to eat for dinner? Explain what this choice suggests about her character.

5   Look again at the final paragraph.

  a   How does the writer use **contrast** here to present Anita and Meena's parents?

  b   How does this contrast influence your view of Anita's character?

Key term

contrast a difference clearly seen when things are compared or seen together

Advanced reading skills

1   Copy and complete the following table to explore how the writer's use of imagery adds to the humour of the text. The first one has been done for you.

Imagery	Effect
'I could have asked mama to tap-dance on top of the telly'	The comic image of Meena's mother tap-dancing on top of the television playing the spoons seems ridiculous and conveys the fevered atmosphere in the house as they await Anita's arrival.
'"What's that!" she demanded, as if confronted with a festering sheep's head on a platter'	
'fearing a culinary cat fight was about to shatter his fragile peace'	
'Anita made a fortress of her arms'	

37

2   What different impressions do you get of Anita and Meena from this text? Use a Venn diagram to display information about both characters, identifying the similarities and differences between them.

Think about:

- each character's actions and the way these are described

- what each character says and the way they speak

- how other characters act towards them.

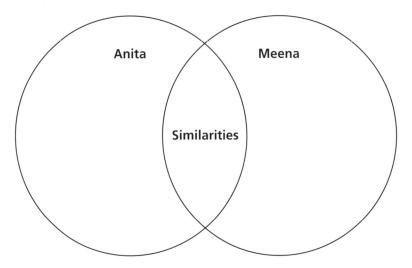

Anita   Meena

Similarities

Key term

extended metaphor
a metaphor which is continued through a series of lines or sentences in a text

3   Why does papa interrupt Anita and mama's conversation about the food? What does this suggest about his character?

4   Find a phrase or sentence in the text that suggests that Meena's mother is offended by Anita's behaviour.

5   The writer creates an **extended metaphor** to describe the way Anita eats her meal. Identify this metaphor and explain what it suggests about Anita's character.

6   This extract features four key characters: Meena, Anita, mama and papa. Which character do you feel most sympathy for at the end of the text? Give reasons for your choice with close reference to the text.

3.2 *A Christmas Carol* by Charles Dickens, 1843

In the following text from Charles Dickens's novella *A Christmas Carol*, the reader is introduced to the protagonist of the story, a rich businessman named Ebenezer Scrooge. As you read, decide what the narrator's attitude towards this character is and think about the techniques he uses to try to persuade the reader to share this view.

Source text 3.2

WORD BANK

covetous having or showing a great desire to possess something that belongs to someone else

gait a person's manner of walking

rime a coating of frost

dog-days the hottest summer days

entreaty an earnest request

handsomely abundantly

gladsome cheerful

trifle a very small amount

courts courtyards

'nuts' slang meaning something agreeable

Scrooge never painted out Old Marley's name. There it stood, years afterwards, above the warehouse door: Scrooge and Marley. The firm was known as Scrooge and Marley. Sometimes people new to the business called Scrooge Scrooge, and sometimes Marley, but he answered to both names. It was all the same to him.

Oh! But he was a tight-fisted hand at the grindstone, Scrooge! a squeezing, wrenching, grasping, scraping, clutching, **covetous**, old sinner! Hard and sharp as flint, from which no steel had ever struck out generous fire; secret, and self-contained, and solitary as an oyster. The cold within him froze his old features, nipped his pointed nose, shrivelled his cheek, stiffened his **gait**; made his eyes red, his thin lips blue; and spoke out shrewdly in his grating voice. A frosty **rime** was on his head, and on his eyebrows, and his wiry chin. He carried his own low temperature always about with him; he iced his office in the **dog-days**; and didn't thaw it one degree at Christmas.

External heat and cold had little influence on Scrooge. No warmth could warm, nor wintry weather chill him. No wind that blew was bitterer than he, no falling snow was more intent upon its purpose, no pelting rain less open to **entreaty**. Foul weather didn't know where to have him. The heaviest rain, and snow, and hail, and sleet, could boast of the advantage over him in only one respect. They often 'came down' **handsomely**, and Scrooge never did.

Nobody ever stopped him in the street to say, with **gladsome** looks, 'My dear Scrooge, how are you? When will you come to see me?' No beggars implored him to bestow a **trifle**, no children asked him what it was o'clock, no man or woman ever once in all his life inquired the way to such and such a place, of Scrooge. Even the blind men's dogs appeared to know him; and when they saw him coming on, would tug their owners into doorways and up **courts**; and then would wag their tails as though they said, 'No eye at all is better than an evil eye, dark master!'

But what did Scrooge care! It was the very thing he liked. To edge his way along the crowded paths of life, warning all human sympathy to keep its distance, was what the knowing ones call **'nuts'** to Scrooge.

1   What is the name of the firm that Ebenezer Scrooge owns?

2   The narrator says that Scrooge has a 'cold within him'. List three ways this affects Scrooge's appearance.

3   Complete the following list of things that Scrooge is never asked for on the street:

   - the time
   - money
   -
   -

4   What kinds of weather is Scrooge compared to?

5   'To edge his way along the crowded paths of life, warning all human sympathy to keep its distance, was what the knowing ones call "nuts" to Scrooge.' Using your own words, explain what this sentence tells you about Scrooge and the way he behaves.

1   Look at the list of adjectives that the narrator uses to describe Scrooge: 'a squeezing, wrenching, grasping, scraping, clutching, covetous, old sinner!'

   a   From this list, choose *one* adjective and explain what impression it gives you of Scrooge's personality.

   b   What effect does listing adjectives in this way have on you as a reader?

2   The author also uses similes to describe Scrooge. Explain what the following similes suggest about Scrooge's character.

   a   '*Hard and sharp as flint*, from which no steel had ever struck out generous fire'

   b   'secret, and self-contained, and *solitary as an oyster*'

3a Choose a word from the list below that best describes Scrooge's character.

mean

aggressive

bitter

selfish

cheerful

3b Select the quotation that you think most effectively conveys your chosen characteristic. Give reasons for your choice.

4 How does the way the writer structures this extract help to build up a picture of Scrooge's character? You should comment on:

- how the character of Scrooge is introduced

- what the focus of each paragraph is and the impression each one gives about Scrooge

- how the beginning of each new paragraph links to the preceding paragraph

- how the extract ends and the final impression this gives you of Scrooge's character.

5 Copy and complete the following character profile for Scrooge to summarize what you have learned about this character from the extract. You should include textual references and quotations as supporting evidence.

Character name:	Ebenezer Scrooge
Distinguishing features:	
Habits/mannerisms:	
Strengths and qualities:	
Weaknesses and flaws:	

6 Both Anita in the extract from *Anita and Me* and Scrooge in the extract from *A Christmas Carol* are unsympathetic characters. Compare the ways these two characters are portrayed. In your comparison you should:

- identify any similarities or differences between Anita and Scrooge

- explore how you respond to each character as a reader

- evaluate which character you think is the most unsympathetic and why.

3.3 *The Lie Tree* by Frances Hardinge, 2015

The following extract is taken from *The Lie Tree* by Frances Hardinge. Set in 1865, the novel is about Faith, a 14-year-old girl who has moved with her family, including her father Reverend Erasmus Sunderly, her mother Myrtle, her younger brother Howard and her Uncle Miles, to the remote island of Vane, in the Channel Islands. Faith's father is a renowned naturalist with a large collection of scientific papers and specimens. Here, Faith and her family are being transported by carriage to the house they have rented in Bull Cove on the island. However the carriage has now come to a halt and Mr Clay, the curate, explains why. As you read, think about the impression you get of the different characters and the relationships between them.

Source text 3.3

'My most profuse apologies. It seems that we have a dilemma. The house you have leased is in Bull Cove, which can only be reached by a low road that follows the shoreline, or by the high track that passes over the ridge and down the other side. I have just learned that the low road is flooded. There is a breakwater, but when the tide is high and the breakers fierce...' He crinkled his forehead and cast an apologetic glance towards the **lowering** sky.

'I assume that the high road is a longer and more **wearisome** journey?' Myrtle asked briskly, with one eye on the morose Howard.

Clay winced. 'It is... a very steep road. Indeed, the driver informs me that the horse would not be equal to it with this carriage in its, ah, current state of burden.'

'Are you suggesting that we will have to get out and *walk?*' Myrtle stiffened, and her small, pretty chin set.

'Mother,' whispered Faith, sensing an **impasse**, 'I have my umbrella, and I do not mind walking a little—'

'No!' snapped Myrtle, just loud enough to make Faith's face redden. 'If I am to become mistress of a new household, I will not make my first appearance looking like a drowned rat. And neither will you!'

Faith felt a rising tide of frustration and anger twisting her innards. She wanted to shout, *What does it matter? The newspapers are tearing us to pieces right now – do you really think people will despise us more if we are wet?*

The curate looked harassed. 'Then I fear the carriage will need to make two journeys. There is an old cabin nearby – a lookout point for spotting sardine shoals. Perhaps your boxes could be left there until the carriage can return for them? I would be happy to stay and watch over them.'

Myrtle's face brightened gratefully, but her answer was cut off by her husband.

WORD BANK

lowering looking dark and threatening

wearisome causing one to feel tired or bored

impasse a situation in which no progress is possible, especially because of disagreement

'Unacceptable,' Faith's father declared. 'Your pardon, but some of these boxes contain irreplaceable flora and fauna that I *must* see installed at the house as soon as possible, lest they perish.'

'Well, I am quite happy to wait in this cabin and spare the horse *my* weight,' declared Uncle Miles.

Clay and Uncle Miles dismounted, and the family's personal trunks and chests were unloaded one by one, leaving only the specimen crates and boxes on the roof. Even then the driver stared at the way the carriage hung down, grimacing and gesturing to indicate it was still too low.

Faith's father made no move to step out and join the other men. 'Erasmus—' began Uncle Miles.

'I must remain with my specimens,' the Reverend interrupted him sharply.

'Perhaps we could leave just one of your crates behind?' enquired Clay. 'There is a box labelled "**miscellaneous** cuttings" which is much heavier than the rest—'

'*No*, Mr Clay.' The Reverend's answer was swift and snow-cold. 'That box is of *particular* importance.'

Faith's father glanced at his family, his eyes cool and distant. His gaze slid over Myrtle and Howard, then settled on Faith. She flushed, knowing that she was being assessed for weight and importance. There was a dipping sensation in her stomach, as if she had been placed in a great set of scales.

Faith felt sick. She could not wait for the mortification of hearing her father voice his decision.

She did not look at her parents as she stood up unsteadily. This time Myrtle said nothing to stop her. Like Faith, she had heard the Reverend's silent decision and had turned meekly to toe the invisible line.

'Miss Sunderly?' Clay was clearly surprised to see Faith climbing out of the carriage, her boots splashing down into a waiting puddle.

'I have an umbrella,' she said quickly, 'and I was hoping for some fresh air.' The little lie left her with a scrap of dignity.

The driver examined the level of his vehicle again and this time nodded. As the carriage rattled away, Faith avoided her companions' eyes, her cheeks hot with humiliation despite the chill wind. She had always known that she was rated less than Howard, the treasured son. Now, however, she knew that she was ranked somewhere below 'miscellaneous cuttings'.

WORD BANK

miscellaneous of various kinds, mixed

Basic reading skills

1 Why does the carriage that Faith is travelling in struggle to get up the hill? Select the correct answer from the options below.

A wheel has fallen off   The carriage is overloaded

The road is flooded   The weather is bad

2 Why can't Faith and her family take the low road to their house in Bull Cove?

3a What reason does Faith's mother give for not wanting to walk to Bull Cove?

3b What impression does this give you about her character?

4a What possible solution does the curate suggest to their transportation problem?

4b How does Faith's father react to the curate's suggestion?

5 Why does Faith decide to climb out of the carriage?

6 Rank the following in order of their importance to Faith's father. Support your chosen rank order with evidence from the text.

Myrtle   His collection of specimens

Faith   Howard

Advanced reading skills

1 What impressions do you get of Faith's father from this extract? Use a spider diagram to collect information about this character under the following categories:

■ action – what Reverend Erasmus does

■ dialogue – what Reverend Erasmus says and how he says it

■ relationships – the way Reverend Erasmus reacts to other characters.

2 Select three textual references that suggest Faith has a difficult relationship with her mother, Myrtle. Explain your choices.

3 Read the section from 'Faith felt sick' to the end of the extract. How does the writer use language to show Faith's emotions in this section? You should comment on the effects created by the writer's use of:

■ descriptive details

■ dialogue

■ the verbs and adjectives chosen to describe Faith's actions.

4 The writer contrasts Faith's inner thoughts and feelings with her outward actions and behaviour. What impression does this contrast give you of Faith's character?

Extended reading

A simple character might have only one distinctive characteristic, while a complex character will have many characteristics.

Choose one of the following characters you have read about in this section and explain whether you think they are a simple or complex character and why.

Anita from *Anita and Me*

Scrooge from *A Christmas Carol*

Faith from *The Lie Tree*

Extended writing

In the course of *A Christmas Carol*, Scrooge changes into a very different character and surprises everyone by embracing the spirit of Christmas. Write a scene which shows how Ebenezer Scrooge's character has changed. You could use the following lines from *A Christmas Carol* to begin your scene:

Source text

'What's to-day?' cried Scrooge, calling downward to a boy in Sunday clothes.
　'Eh?' returned the boy, with all his might of wonder.

As you write, think about:

- Scrooge's attitude to the boy and how you can suggest this
- what will happen in the scene and how you can show Scrooge's change of character through his thoughts, actions and dialogue
- the language choices you make to describe Scrooge, such as the use of similes and metaphor
- how you can structure the scene in a way that helps the reader to understand how Scrooge has changed.

Remember to check the spelling, punctuation and grammar of your writing.

Early bird

When you write, you can show a character's thoughts and emotions in the way you describe their actions. Write one sentence describing a teenager leaving a classroom in a way that shows each of the following emotions:

- anger   ■ fear   ■ happiness   ■ hope   ■ surprise

Compare the five sentences you have written and discuss the choices you made in each one to suggest the different emotions.

Source texts table

Text	Date
4.1 *Frankenstein* by Mary Shelley	1818
4.2 'The Night' by Ray Bradbury	1946
4.3 'To Build a Fire' by Jack London	1908

Big picture

When you read fiction, you step into other lives and experience new worlds from different perspectives. Every story is told from a point of view. This might be from the perspective of a character in the story, with every scene seen through their eyes. Or perhaps the **narrator** is an observer of the events of the story rather than a character directly involved in the action. What viewpoints are some of your favourite stories told from? In this section you will read extracts from novels and short stories that are told from different **narrative viewpoints** and explore the effects these create.

Skills

- Understand the meaning of a text

- Make inferences and refer to evidence in the text

- Study the effects created by the use of different narrative viewpoints

- Comment on a writer's use of language

- Experiment with different narrative viewpoints in your own fiction writing

Before reading

Key terms

narrator the person or character who recounts the events of a story

narrative viewpoint the perspective a story is told from, for example, first person

1   Look at the following extracts and match them to the narrative viewpoint they are written from, using the information from the table below.

   a Elise sighed as she remembered how she had cared for Steven before his betrayal. But Steven just turned away, unable even to meet her gaze.

   b I knew it was going to be a bad day from the moment I got out of bed and stepped on a Lego brick.

   c You never know how hard it will be to leave until the moment comes to say goodbye.

Narrative viewpoint	Definition	Features
First person	Where the narrator is a character in the story, usually the protagonist.	Uses first-person pronouns such as 'I' and 'we'
Second person	Where the narrator is a character in the story and refers to himself or herself in the second person. In fiction, the second-person viewpoint is rarely used.	Uses the second-person pronoun 'you'
Third person	Where the narrator is not a character, but an observer of the events of the story. This narrator may have knowledge of all characters and their thoughts or just know everything about one particular character.	Uses third-person pronouns such as 'he', 'she', 'it' or 'they'

2 Look at the following reason one student has given for preferring stories written from a first-person viewpoint:

You feel connected to the protagonist of the story.

Do you prefer stories that are written from a first-person or third-person viewpoint? Give reasons for your choice.

4.1 *Frankenstein* by Mary Shelley, 1818

The following text is taken from the novel *Frankenstein* by Mary Shelley about a scientist named Victor Frankenstein who creates a monster. Here, after deserting the monster, Victor has returned to his hometown of Geneva and learned that his younger brother William has been murdered in mysterious circumstances. As you read, think about how the first-person viewpoint allows you to share Victor's emotions.

Source text 4.1

WORD BANK

environs the surrounding districts

promontory a piece of high land that sticks out into a sea or a lake

It was completely dark when I arrived in the **environs** of Geneva; the gates of the town were already shut; and I was obliged to pass the night at Secheron, a village at the distance of half a league from the city. The sky was serene; and, as I was unable to rest, I resolved to visit the spot where my poor William had been murdered. As I could not pass through the town, I was obliged to cross the lake in a boat to arrive at Plainpalais. During this short voyage I saw the lightnings playing on the summit of Mont Blanc in the most beautiful figures. The storm appeared to approach rapidly; and, on landing, I ascended a low hill, that I might observe its progress. It advanced; the heavens were clouded, and I soon felt the rain coming slowly in large drops, but its violence quickly increased.

I quitted my seat, and walked on, although the darkness and storm increased every minute, and the thunder burst with a terrific crash over my head. It was echoed from Salêve, the Juras, and the Alps of Savoy; vivid flashes of lightning dazzled my eyes, illuminating the lake, making it appear like a vast sheet of fire; then for an instant everything seemed of a pitchy darkness, until the eye recovered itself from the preceding flash. The storm, as is often the case in Switzerland, appeared at once in various parts of the heavens. The most violent storm hung exactly north of the town, over that part of the lake which lies between the **promontory** of Belrive and the village of Copêt. Another storm enlightened Jura with faint flashes; and another darkened and sometimes disclosed the Môle, a peaked mountain to the east of the lake.

WORD BANK

tempest a violent storm

elevated lifted or raised up

thy your

dirge a slow sad song, the first word of a song used in the Roman Catholic service for a dead person

daemon demon

While I watched the **tempest**, so beautiful yet terrific, I wandered on with a hasty step. This noble war in the sky **elevated** my spirits; I clasped my hands, and exclaimed aloud, 'William, dear angel this is **thy** funeral, this thy **dirge!**' As I said these words, I perceived in the gloom a figure which stole from behind a clump of trees near me; I stood fixed, gazing intently: I could not be mistaken. A flash of lightning illuminated the object, and discovered its shape plainly to me; its gigantic stature, and the deformity of its aspect, more hideous than belongs to humanity, instantly informed me that it was the wretch, the filthy **daemon**, to whom I had given life. What did he there? Could he be (I shuddered at the conception) the murderer of my brother? No sooner did that idea cross my imagination, than I became convinced of its truth; my teeth chattered, and I was forced to lean against a tree for support.

Basic reading skills

1 Re-read the first paragraph.

   a What information does the narrator give the reader about:

   - the time at which the events take place

   - the locations Victor visits

   - the weather?

   b Why does Victor decide to visit the spot where his brother was murdered?

   c Why does he cross the lake rather than pass through the town of Geneva to reach this spot?

   d Why does Victor decide to climb a low hill?

2 Now look again at the second paragraph. List three details that Victor gives that show the violence of the storm.

3 In the final paragraph, where does Victor first see the figure of the monster?

4 Look again at the final sentence. Why does Victor have to lean against a tree for support?

Advanced reading skills

1 In a first-person narrative, a writer's choice of vocabulary and descriptive details can suggest the narrator's thoughts and feelings towards different characters and events.

   a In the final paragraph, the narrator refers to the creature as a 'wretch'. In your own words, say what you think this means.

   b Explain what the choice of the word 'wretch' suggests about the narrator's feelings towards the creature.

   c Select three more textual details used to describe the creature and explain what these suggest about the narrator's feelings towards it.

2 When describing the storm, Victor says, 'This noble war in the sky elevated my spirits'.

   Using your own words, explain what he means by this.

3 Re-read the final paragraph.

   a Choose one word from the list below that best describes Victor Frankenstein's mood at the start of the paragraph and one word that best describes his mood at the end of the paragraph.

   horrified   **forgetful**   **proud**

   nervous   **weary**   **triumphant**

   b Write a sentence explaining how Victor Frankenstein's mood at the end of the paragraph contrasts with his mood at the start.

4 Choose the statement below that you most agree with and complete it in your own words.

   I like the fact that this extract is told from a first-person viewpoint because...

   I dislike the fact this extract is told from a first-person viewpoint because...

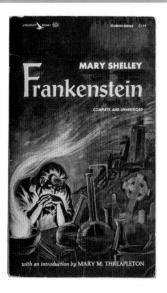

4.2 'The Night' by Ray Bradbury, 1946

The following text is taken from 'The Night', a short story by the American writer Ray Bradbury. Here, as night falls, an eight-year-old boy who is nicknamed Shorts and his mother are awaiting the return of the boy's older brother Skipper, who has been out playing with his friends on the other side of town. As you read, think about the narrative viewpoint the story is told from and the effect this creates.

Source text 4.2

You sit enjoying the ice cream. You are at the core of the deep quiet summer night. Your mother and yourself and the night all around this small house on this small street. You lick each spoon of ice cream thoroughly before digging for another, and Mom puts her ironing board away and the hot iron in its case, and she sits in the armchair by the phonograph, eating her dessert and saying, 'My lands, it was a hot day today. It's still hot. Earth soaks up all the heat and lets it out at night. It'll be soggy sleeping.'

You both sit there listening to the summer silence. The dark is pressed down by every window and door, there is no sound because the radio needs a new battery, and you have played all the Knickerbocker Quartet records and Al Jolson and Two Black Crows records to exhaustion; so you just sit on the hardwood floor by the door and look out into the dark dark dark, pressing your nose against the screen until the flesh of its tip is moulded into small dark squares.

'I wonder where your brother is?' Mother says after a while. Her spoon scrapes on the dish. 'He should be home by now. It's almost nine-thirty.'

'He'll be here,' you say, knowing very well that he will be.

You follow Mom out to wash the dishes. Each sound, each rattle of spoon or dish is amplified in the baked evening. Silently, you go to the

living room, remove the couch cushions and, together, yank it open
and extend it down into the double bed that it secretly is. Mother makes
the bed, punching pillows neatly to flump them up for your head.
Then, as you are unbuttoning your shirt, she says:

'Wait awhile, Doug.'

'Why?'

'Because. I say so.'

'You look funny, Mom.'

Mom sits down a moment, then stands up, goes to the door,
and calls. You listen to her calling and calling Skipper, Skipper,
Skiiiiiiiiperrrrrrrr over and over. Her calling goes out into the summer-
warm dark and never comes back. The echoes pay no attention.

Skipper. Skipper. Skipper.

Skipper!

And as you sit on the floor a coldness that is not ice cream and not
winter, and not part of summer's heat, goes through you. You notice
Mom's eyes sliding, blinking; the way she stands undecided and is
nervous. All of these things.

She opens the screen door. Stepping out into the night she walks
down the steps and down the front sidewalk under the lilac bush. You
listen to her moving feet.

She calls again. Silence.

She calls twice more. You sit in the room. Any moment now Skipper
will reply, from down the long long narrow street:

'All right, Mom! All right, Mother! Hey!'

But he doesn't answer. And for two minutes you sit looking at the
made-up bed, the silent radio, the silent phonograph, at the chandelier
with its crystal bobbins gleaming quietly, at the rug with the scarlet
and purple curlicues on it. You stub your toe on the bed purposely to
see if it hurts. It does.

Whining, the screen door opens, and Mother says:

'Come on, Shorts. We'll take a walk.'

'Where to?'

'Just down the block. Come on. Better put your shoes on, though.
You'll catch cold.'

'No, I won't. I'll be all right.'

You take her hand. Together you walk down St. James Street. You
smell roses in blossom, fallen apples lying crushed and odorous in the
deep grass. Underfoot, the concrete is still warm, and the crickets are
sounding louder against the darkening dark. You reach a corner, turn,
and walk toward the ravine.

Basic reading skills

1 In the opening paragraph the narrator's mother says, 'My lands, it was a hot day today. It's still hot.' Select another detail from this paragraph that suggests that it is still hot.

2 What is the first sign that the narrator's mother is worried about Skipper's whereabouts?

3 Why does the narrator's mother stop him from unbuttoning his shirt when he is getting ready for bed?

4 Find a phrase or sentence in the text that suggests the narrator is worried about Skipper.

5 Where do the narrator and his mother walk towards after they leave the house?

Advanced reading skills

1 Unusually, this story is narrated from a second-person viewpoint. Choose the statement below that you most agree with and finish it off in your own words:

> The second-person viewpoint makes the story feel more sinister because...

> The second-person viewpoint gives the story a sense of urgency because...

> The second-person viewpoint makes me feel involved in the story because...

2 Why do you think the narrator stubs his toe on the bed? Explain why you think the writer has included this detail.

3 Look again at the final paragraph.

You take her hand. Together you walk down St. James Street. You smell roses in blossom, fallen apples lying crushed and odorous in the deep grass. Underfoot, the concrete is still warm, and the crickets are sounding louder against the darkening dark. You reach a corner, turn, and walk toward the ravine.

a Rewrite this paragraph from a first-person viewpoint and in the past tense, for example:

I took my mother's hand. Together we walked...

b Compare these two versions. Which do you prefer and why? Justify your choice with an explanation of the different effects created by each version.

4 What do you think might happen next in the story?

4.3 'To Build a Fire' by Jack London, 1908

The following text is taken from 'To Build a Fire', a short story by the American writer Jack London, which describes how a man out trekking with his husky dog in the freezing Canadian wilderness becomes badly frostbitten. Here, the man is desperately attempting to build and light a fire in order to save his own life. As you read, think about what impression you get of the man.

Source text 4.3

WORD BANK

birch-bark the bark of a birch-tree, commonly used as a fire-starter

When all was ready, the man reached in his pocket for a second piece of **birch-bark**. He knew the bark was there, and, though he could not feel it with his fingers, he could hear its crisp rustling as he fumbled for it. Try as he would, he could not clutch hold of it. And all the time, in his consciousness, was the knowledge that each instant his feet were freezing. This thought tended to put him in a panic, but he fought against it and kept calm. He pulled on his mittens with his teeth, and threshed his arms back and forth, beating his hands with all his might against his sides. He did this sitting down, and he stood up to do it; and all the while the dog sat in the snow, its wolf-brush of a tail curled around warmly over its forefeet, its sharp wolf-ears pricked forward intently as it watched the man. And the man, as he beat and threshed with his arms and hands, felt a great surge of envy as he regarded the creature that was warm and secure in its natural covering.

After a time he was aware of the first faraway signals of sensation in his beaten fingers. The faint tingling grew stronger till it evolved into a stinging ache that was excruciating, but which the man hailed with satisfaction. He stripped the mitten from his right hand and fetched forth the birch-bark. The exposed fingers were quickly going numb again. Next he brought out his bunch of sulphur matches. But the tremendous cold had already driven the life out of his fingers. In his effort to separate one match from the others, the whole bunch fell in the snow. He tried to pick it out of the snow, but failed. The dead fingers could neither touch nor clutch. He was very careful. He drove

the thought of his freezing feet, and nose, and cheeks, out of his mind, devoting his whole soul to the matches. He watched, using the sense of vision in place of that of touch, and when he saw his fingers on each side the bunch, he closed them—that is, he willed to close them, for the wires were down, and the fingers did not obey. He pulled the mitten on the right hand, and beat it fiercely against his knee. Then, with both mittened hands, he scooped the bunch of matches, along with much snow, into his lap. Yet he was no better off.

After some manipulation he managed to get the bunch between the heels of his mittened hands. In this fashion he carried it to his mouth. The ice crackled and snapped when by a violent effort he opened his mouth. He drew the lower jaw in, curled the upper lip out of the way, and scraped the bunch with his upper teeth in order to separate a match. He succeeded in getting one, which he dropped on his lap. He was no better off. He could not pick it up. Then he devised a way. He picked it up in his teeth and scratched it on his leg. Twenty times he scratched before he succeeded in lighting it. As it flamed he held it with his teeth to the birch-bark. But the burning brimstone went up his nostrils and into his lungs, causing him to cough spasmodically. The match fell into the snow and went out.

The old-timer on Sulphur Creek was right, he thought in the moment of controlled despair that ensued: after fifty below, a man should travel with a partner. He beat his hands, but failed in exciting any sensation. Suddenly he bared both hands, removing the mittens with his teeth. He caught the whole bunch between the heels of his hands. His arm-muscles not being frozen enabled him to press the hand-heels tightly against the matches. Then he scratched the bunch along his leg. It flared into flame, seventy sulphur matches at once! There was no wind to blow them out. He kept his head to one side to escape the strangling fumes, and held the blazing bunch to the birch-bark. As he so held it, he became aware of sensation in his hand. His flesh was burning. He could smell it. Deep down below the surface he could feel it. The sensation developed into pain that grew acute. And still he endured it, holding the flame of the matches clumsily to the bark that would not light readily because his own burning hands were in the way, absorbing most of the flame.

At last, when he could endure no more, he jerked his hands apart. The blazing matches fell sizzling into the snow, but the birch-bark was alight. He began laying dry grasses and the tiniest twigs on the flame. He could not pick and choose, for he had to lift the fuel between the heels of his hands. Small pieces of rotten wood and green moss clung to the twigs, and he bit them off as well as he could with his teeth. He cherished the flame carefully and awkwardly. It meant life, and it must not perish. The withdrawal of blood from the surface of his body now made him begin to shiver, and he grew more awkward. A large piece of green moss fell squarely on the little fire. He tried to poke it out with his fingers, but his shivering frame made him poke too far, and he disrupted the nucleus of the little fire, the burning grasses and tiny twigs separating and scattering. He tried to poke them together again, but in spite of the tenseness of the effort, his shivering got away with him, and the twigs were hopelessly scattered. Each twig gushed a puff of smoke and went out.

Basic reading skills

1 Re-read the opening paragraph. How does the man know that a piece of birch-bark is in his pocket?

2 List three things the man does to try to get sensation back into his frostbitten fingers.

3 Why does the man feel 'a great surge of envy' as he looks at his dog?

4 When the man attempts to pick up the fallen bunch of matches, Jack London writes, 'the wires were down, and the fingers did not obey'. Explain in your own words what you think this means.

5 What had the old-timer on Sulphur Creek told the man about travelling when the temperature is colder than fifty below?

6 Why do you think the words 'fingers', 'mittens', 'matches' and 'flame' are repeated throughout the extract? What effect does this repetition create?

Advanced reading skills

1   Look again at the third paragraph. In your own words, describe what the man does in this section to try to light the fire.

2   Now re-read the fourth paragraph. How does the way the writer describes the man's actions show his desperation to survive?

3   How does the writer build tension in the fifth paragraph? Comment on the writer's use of language and sentence forms and how these help to create a tense atmosphere.

4   Choose the statement below that you most agree with and finish it off in your own words. Refer to details in the text to support your statement.

> The author makes the reader feel sympathetic towards the protagonist by...

> The author makes the reader feel the protagonist is foolish by...

Extended reading

Choose two of the extracts you have read in this section and compare how the writers convey an impression of their protagonist. Use some or all of these questions to structure your response.

■   What narrative viewpoint is each extract told from and what effects does this create?

■   How do the authors establish their protagonist and make the reader interested in him?

■   What are the feelings or attitude of each protagonist and how are these shown?

■   Does each writer's use of language and sentence forms help to convey an impression of the protagonist?

■   How does the way each extract is structured contribute to the impression given of the protagonist?

Extended writing

Write about the following incident from two different narrative viewpoints.

A character who is waiting alone at a bus stop is mugged by a stranger.

You can choose to write this incident from a first-person viewpoint (narrated by either the character who is waiting or the stranger), a second-person viewpoint, or a third-person viewpoint. Think about how you can draw on the techniques you have explored in the extracts you have read in this section to create an engaging scene.

Discuss your finished work with a partner and ask them to choose which they prefer.

Early bird

Rewrite these famous opening lines from fiction from a different narrative viewpoint.

'Hale knew, before he had been in Brighton three hours, that they meant to murder him.' Brighton Rock by Graham Greene

'Last night I dreamt I went to Manderley again. It seemed to me I stood by the iron gate leading to the drive, and for a while I could not enter, for the way was barred to me.' Rebecca by Daphne Du Maurier

'One morning, when Gregor Samsa woke from troubled dreams, he found himself transformed in his bed into a horrible vermin.' Metamorphosis by Franz Kafka

'In my younger and more vulnerable years my father gave me some advice that I've been turning over in my mind ever since.' The Great Gatsby by F. Scott Fitzgerald

Choose your favourite original opening line. Do you prefer any of the alternative versions?

Source texts table

Text	Date
5.1 *Into That Forest* by Louis Nowra	2013
5.2 *Never Let Me Go* by Kazuo Ishiguro	2005
5.3 *Jane Eyre* by Charlotte Brontë	1847

Big picture

Sometimes when you read a story you can hear a voice inside your mind. This might be the voice of the character who is telling the story or the voice of the writer who has created the tale. The narrative voice that you hear can reveal a narrator's character or personality, create a specific mood and atmosphere, and also influence the way you respond to the story as a reader. What narrative voices have stuck in your head from the stories you have read? In this section you'll read extracts from three novels and explore the techniques their authors use to create distinctive narrative voices.

Skills

- Understand the meaning of a text

- Make inferences and refer to evidence in the text

- Explore how writers create a narrative voice

- Practise creating a distinctive narrative voice in your own fiction writing

Before reading

In a story written from a first-person viewpoint, the narrator is usually the protagonist of the story. In order to create a convincing narrative voice, a writer has to carefully consider the kind of language this character would use to describe events and express their emotions.

1 Match the examples of different narrative voices below to the narrator they belong to.

Narrative voice

1. Indisposed to hesitate, my eye sought out Mr Rogers across the crowded ballroom, his passing glance sending my soul and senses quivering with keen throes.

2. As soon as the dame walked into the joint, I could tell that this case was going to be trouble.

3. Error! Primary objective overridden. New orders received. Eliminate all flesh units.

4. I knows I shouldn't have been ear-creeping at the door, but them botherers had been hornswoggling me for days.

5. The scent of danger hung in the air like cheap perfume, but my mind was as calm as a frozen lake as I drew my service revolver.

Narrators

a. A British secret agent

b. An android from the year 3000

c. A young Victorian lady

d. A private detective

e. A cabin boy aboard a 19th-century ship

5.1 *Into That Forest* by Louis Nowra, 2013

The following text is taken from the opening to the novel *Into That Forest* by Louis Nowra. Here the narrator Hannah introduces herself to the reader. As you read, think about what impression you get of her.

Source text 5.1

WORD BANK

Tasmania island state to the south of the Australian mainland

backblocks outback, remote and sparsely populated area

yabber slang for talk or chatter

Me name be Hannah O'Brien and I be seventy-six years old. Me first thing is an apology – me language is bad cos I lost it and had to learn it again. But here's me story and I be glad to tell it before I hop the twig.

I were born in **Tasmania**, born not in a hospital but here in the **backblocks**. In this actual house. It is crumbling round me ears now, but the roof hardly leaks and if I chop enough wood I can heat the place when it snows. Though I live here by meself I am not lonely. I got a wedding photograph of me mother and me father when men wore beards and sat down for the picture while me mother wears a wedding dress and stands beside him. And there's me father's harpoon hanging from the living room wall with its cracked wooden handle and rusted blade. Me only new thing is the cabinet with a radio in it which Mr Dixon down at the general store gave me. I can't hack it. There always be mongrel music in it, like it's shouting all the time. Anyway, I'd sooner **yabber** to meself than listen to those voices inside that box. I reckon I need new curtains, these are a bit dusty and fraying, but they keep out the summer light when it's so strong it hurts me eyes.

I think me uncle built this house. He gave it to me father. It were a present. At that time we were the only house for miles and miles. Me father wanted to live in a place near water – if not the sea, then a river. Me mother liked rivers and so the house were a give-and-take for the both of them. From the verandah we could almost touch the Munro River as it flowed down to the sea. I had no brothers or sisters. I don't know why. There were a problem, I think. I'd hear me mother crying buckets in me father's arms and hear him say, like to a child, *There, there, we got Hannah.*

Basic reading skills

1 Why does the narrator apologize to the reader?

2 The narrator says she will be glad to tell her story 'before I hop the twig'. What do you think this slang phrase means in this context?

3 List five details about the narrator's house. One has been given below:

■ Hannah's house is located in the Tasmanian outback.

4 How does the writer suggest to the reader that Hannah's parents wanted to have more children?

Advanced reading skills

1 What are your first impressions of Hannah? Identify any specific details from the text that contribute to this impression.

2a How would you describe the narrator's tone of voice? You could choose a word from the list below or suggest your own.

cheerful resilient accepting sentimental nostalgic self-aware

Key term

non-standard personal pronouns
not of the form that is accepted as standard, that is, 'me uncle' instead of 'my uncle'

2b Select the three quotations that you think most effectively contribute to creating this tone of voice. Give reasons for your choices.

3 Read this comment on the text and decide whether you agree or disagree with it:

Even though the narrator is seventy-six years old, the narrative voice is quite childlike.

a Find two details from the text that support this view.

b What, if anything, in the text would make you disagree with this view?

4 How does the writer create a distinctive narrative voice? You should comment on the effects created by the writer's use of:

■ **non-standard personal pronouns**

■ slang words and phrases such as 'hop the twig'

■ sentence lengths and structures.

5 Re-read the final paragraph. How do you think the writer wants you to feel towards Hannah here? Refer to relevant details from this paragraph to support your answer.

5.2 *Never Let Me Go* by Kazuo Ishiguro, 2005

The following text is taken from the opening of the science-fiction novel *Never Let Me Go* by Kazuo Ishiguro. Here the narrator Kathy describes her role as a carer who looks after donors.

Source text 5.2

My name is Kathy H. I'm thirty-one years old, and I've been a carer now for over eleven years. That sounds long enough, I know, but actually they want me to go on for another eight months, until the end of this year. That'll make it almost exactly twelve years. Now I know my being a carer so long isn't necessarily because they think I'm fantastic at what I do. There are some really good carers who've been told to stop after just two or three years. And I can think of one carer at least who went on for all of fourteen years despite being a complete waste of space. So I'm not trying to boast. But then I do know for a fact they've been pleased with my work, and by and large, I have too. My donors have always tended to do much better than expected. Their recovery times have been impressive, and hardly any of them have been classified as 'agitated', even before fourth donation. Okay, maybe I *am* boasting now. But it means a lot to me, being able to do my work well, especially that bit about my donors staying 'calm'. I've developed a kind of instinct around donors. I know when to hang around and comfort them, when to leave them to themselves; when to listen to everything they have to say, and when just to shrug and tell them to snap out of it.

Anyway, I'm not making any big claims for myself. I know carers, working now, who are just as good and don't get half the credit. If you're one of them, I can understand how you might get resentful—about my bedsit, my car, above all, the way I get to pick and choose who I look after. And I'm a Hailsham student—which is enough by itself sometimes to get people's backs up. Kathy H., they say, she gets to pick and choose, and she always chooses her own kind: people from Hailsham, or one of the other privileged estates. No wonder she has a great record. I've heard it said enough, so I'm sure you've heard it plenty more, and maybe there's something in it. But I'm not the first to be allowed to pick and choose, and I doubt if I'll be the last. And anyway, I've done my share of looking after donors brought up in every kind of place. By the time I finish, remember, I'll have done twelve years of this, and it's only for the last six they've let me choose.

And why shouldn't they? Carers aren't machines. You try and do your best for every donor, but in the end, it wears you down. You don't have unlimited patience and energy. So when you get a chance to choose, of course, you choose your own kind. That's natural. There's no way I could have gone on for as long as I have if I'd stopped feeling for my donors every step of the way. And anyway, if I'd never started choosing, how would I ever have got close again to Ruth and Tommy after all those years?

Basic reading skills

1   How old is the narrator?

2   For how long does Kathy say she's been a 'carer'?

3   Choose one word from the list below to describe how Kathy feels about her role as a carer:

proud   bored   fantastic

worried   agitated

Write a sentence explaining your choice.

4   Re-read the second paragraph. Why does Kathy suggest that other carers resent her? Pick out the evidence she presents to support this statement.

5   'Carers aren't machines.' In your own words, explain what you think this statement means.

Advanced reading skills

1 What are your first impressions of Kathy? Identify any specific details from the text that contribute to this impression.

2 Read what this student says about the text:

Kathy's narrative voice is rather ordinary and has a conversational tone.

Can you identify any evidence to support this statement? You could comment on the effects created by the writer's use of:

- clichés such as 'complete waste of space'

- direct address to the reader

- vocabulary and sentence forms.

3 As a 'carer', Kathy looks after human beings who have been cloned and bred for organ donation. Does this knowledge change the way you respond to Kathy as a narrator? Explain your answer with reference to the language Kathy uses to describe her role as a 'carer'.

4 Compare the extracts from *Into That Forest* and *Never Let Me Go*. In your comparison you should:

- identify any similarities and differences between the narrative voices and the techniques used to create these

- explore how you respond to each narrative voice as a reader

- evaluate which narrative voice you think is the most successful and why.

5.3 *Jane Eyre* by Charlotte Brontë, 1847

The following extract is taken from the novel *Jane Eyre* by Charlotte Brontë. Jane, the narrator, has discovered that the man she is in love with and was due to marry, Mr Rochester, already has a wife. She has fled their home at Thornfield and is now sleeping outdoors and forced to beg for food. As you read, think about how the writer shows Jane's feelings about her situation.

Source text 5.3

A little before dark I passed a farm-house, at the open door of which the farmer was sitting, eating his supper of bread and cheese; I stopped and said:—

'Will you give me a piece of bread? for I am very hungry.' He cast on me a glance of surprise; but without answering, he cut a thick slice from his loaf, and gave it to me. I imagine he did not think I was a beggar, but only an eccentric sort of lady, who had taken a fancy to his brown loaf. As soon as I was out of sight of his house, I sat down and ate it.

I could not hope to get a **lodging** under a roof, and sought it in the wood I have before **alluded to**. But my night was wretched, my rest broken: the ground was damp, the air cold: besides, intruders passed near me more than once, and I had again and again to change my quarters: no sense of safety or tranquillity befriended me. Towards morning it rained; the whole of the following day was wet. Do not ask me, reader, to give a minute account of that day: as before, I sought work; as before, I was repulsed; as before, I starved: but once did food pass my lips. At the door of a cottage I saw a little girl about to throw a mess of cold porridge into a pig trough. 'Will you give me that?' I asked.

She stared at me. 'Mother!' she exclaimed, 'there is a woman wants me to give her these porridge.'

'Well lass,' replied a voice within, 'give it her if she's a beggar. T' pig doesn't want it.'

The girl emptied the stiffened mould into my hand, and I devoured it ravenously.

As the wet twilight deepened, I stopped in a solitary **bridle-path**, which I had been pursuing an hour or more.

'My strength is quite failing me,' I said in **soliloquy**. 'I feel I cannot go much further. Shall I be an outcast again this night? While the rain descends so, must I lay my head on the cold, drenched ground? I fear I cannot do otherwise: for who will receive me? But it will be very dreadful: with this feeling of hunger, faintness, chill, and this sense of desolation—this total **prostration** of hope. In all likelihood, though, I should die before morning. And why cannot I **reconcile** myself to

WORD BANK

lodging a room or rooms

alluded to mentioned briefly or indirectly

bridle-path a road suitable for horses, but not for vehicles

soliloquy a dramatic speech in which a person speaks their inner thoughts aloud when alone or without addressing anyone

prostration total exhaustion, collapse

reconcile accept an unwelcome fact or situation

the prospect of death? Why do I struggle to retain a valueless life? Because I know, or believe Mr. Rochester is living: and then, to die of want and cold, is a fate to which nature cannot submit passively. Oh, **Providence**! sustain me a little longer! Aid—direct me!'

My glazed eye wandered over the dim and misty landscape. I saw I had strayed far from the village: it was quite out of sight. The very cultivation surrounding it had disappeared. I had, by cross-ways and by-paths, once more drawn near the tract of moorland; and now, only a few fields, almost as wild and unproductive as the heath from which they were scarcely reclaimed, lay between me and the dusky hill.

'Well; I would rather die **yonder** than in a street or on a frequented road," I reflected. "And far better that crows and ravens—if any ravens there be in these regions—should pick my flesh from my bones, than that they should be prisoned in a **workhouse** coffin and moulder in a **pauper's** grave.'

To the hill, then, I turned. I reached it. It remained now only to find a hollow where I could lie down, and feel at least hidden, if not secure: but all the surface of the waste looked level. It showed no variation but of tint: green, where rush and moss overgrew the marshes; black, where the dry soil bore only heath. Dark as it was getting, I could still see these changes; though but as mere alternations of light and shade: for colour had faded with the daylight.

My eye still roved over the sullen swell, and along the moor-edge, vanishing amidst the wildest scenery; when at one dim point, far in among the marshes and the ridges, a light sprang up.

WORD BANK

Providence the care and protection given by God or nature

yonder over there

workhouse an institution where people unable to support themselves were housed in return for work

pauper a person who is very poor

Basic reading skills

1 What two things does Jane eat in this extract? How does she get these items of food?

2a Where does Jane sleep in this extract?

2b 'My night was wretched, my rest broken.' In your own words, explain what this sentence means in this context.

2c List three details that explain why Jane's 'night was wretched' and her 'rest broken'.

3 Write down two or three details from the text that suggest it is not set in the modern day.

4 Re-read the paragraph beginning '"My strength is quite failing me," I said in soliloquy.' What is the main fear that Jane expresses about her situation here? Choose one of the statements below, giving reasons for your choice.

    a She will be forced to sleep outside again.

    b She is worried that Mr Rochester will find her.

    c She can't bear to die knowing that Mr Rochester is alive.

    d She believes her life is worthless without Mr Rochester.

5 Re-read the section beginning 'My glazed eye wandered over the dim and misty landscape' to the end of the text. Choose three details that make it seem like a sinister and threatening landscape.

Advanced reading skills

1 Look at the character of the narrator. What impressions do you get of Jane Eyre from this extract? Use a spider diagram to collect all the information you can about her from the text.

2 Look again at the paragraph beginning '"My strength is quite failing me," I said in soliloquy.' Explain what the different sentence forms and types used in this paragraph suggest about her thoughts and feelings at this point in the story.

3a Why does Jane think it would be better to die out on the moor than on a street or a road?

3b How does this make you feel towards her as a character?

4 Read what this student says about the narrative voice in this extract:

I think the author creates a **melodramatic** narrative voice.

Explain what you think the student means and then say whether you agree or disagree with their statement. Justify your answer with reference to the text.

5 What do you predict might happen next in the story?

Key terms

melodramatic characteristic of melodrama, especially in being exaggerated or over-emotional

pathetic fallacy a literary technique where a character's emotions are reflected or represented by the environment or landscape

Extended reading

Pathetic fallacy is a literary technique where a character's emotions are reflected or represented by the environment or landscape. Re-read the introduction to the extract from *Jane Eyre* and the text itself.

How does the author's description of the landscape in this text reflect Jane's emotional state? You could comment on the effects created by:

■ the writer's choice of vocabulary

■ the choice of sentence types and forms

■ the way the description is structured, that is, where the reader's attention is focused and how this changes.

Extended writing

Write a description of the following location in the narrative voice of one of the narrators from the extracts you have read in this section: Hannah from *Into That Forest*, Kathy from *Never Let Me Go* or Jane from *Jane Eyre*.

As you write, think about:

■ how your choices of vocabulary and sentence forms can help to create this narrative voice

■ the features and details your chosen narrator would focus on and how they would describe them

■ your narrator's attitude to the location and how you can suggest this.

Remember to check the spelling, punctuation and grammar of your writing.

Early bird

Can you solve this riddle?

> I have no voice yet I speak to you. I tell of all the things in the world that people do.
>
> I have leaves, but I am not a tree.
>
> I have pages, but I am not a bride.
>
> I have a spine and hinges, but I am not a man or a door.
>
> I have told you all, I cannot tell you more.
>
> Who am I?

Now make up your own riddle and challenge someone else to solve it.

Source texts table

Text	Date
6.1 *Wonder* by R. J. Palacio	2012
6.2 *The Invisible Man* by H. G. Wells	1897
6.3 *The Day of the Triffids* by John Wyndham	1951

Big picture

Have you ever given up reading a novel or short story before you even finished the first page? If you have, what was it that made you give up? Maybe the start of the story didn't grab your attention. Or did you discover that the novel was in a different genre to the one you were expecting? In this section you'll read the openings from three different novels and explore the techniques different writers use to 'hook' their readers.

Skills

- Understand the meaning of a text
- Make inferences and refer to evidence in the text
- Study how setting, plot and characterization are established
- Draft the opening of a narrative that engages the reader

Before reading

1 Think about any novels you have read recently. What happened at the start of the story? Give it a rating to indicate how much it made you want to read on. Copy and complete the table below to record your ideas.

Title of novel and author's name	How did it begin?	'Read on' rating (1–5 with 5 being very keen to read on)

2 Look at the following statements from the author John Braine:

   'A good beginning means a good book.'

   'A good beginning is one which takes the reader straight into the action.'

   'A good beginning must tell us who and what the novel will be about.'

How far do you agree with each statement? Discuss your ideas, referring to novels and stories you have read.

3 Write your own short statement explaining what you think makes an effective opening.

6.1 *Wonder* by R.J. Palacio, 2012

The following text is the opening of a novel called *Wonder* by R. J. Palacio. As you read, think about how effective this opening is.

Source text 6.1

I know I'm not an ordinary ten-year-old kid. I mean, sure, I do ordinary things. I eat ice cream. I ride my bike. I play ball. I have an XBox. Stuff like that makes me ordinary. I guess. And I feel ordinary. Inside. But I know ordinary kids don't make other ordinary kids run away screaming in playgrounds. I know ordinary kids don't get stared at wherever they go.

If I found a magic lamp and I could have one wish, I would wish that I had a normal face that no one ever noticed at all. I would wish that I could walk down the street without people seeing me and then doing that look-away thing. Here's what I think: the only reason I'm not ordinary is that no one else sees me that way.

But I'm kind of used to how I look by now. I know how to pretend I don't see the faces people make. We've all gotten pretty good at that sort of thing: me, Mom and Dad, Via. Actually, I take that back: Via's not so good at it. She can get really annoyed when people do something rude. Like, for instance, one time in the playground some older kids made some noises. I don't even know what the noises were exactly because I didn't hear them myself, but Via heard and she just started yelling at the kids. That's the way she is. I'm not that way.

Via doesn't see me as ordinary. She says she does, but if I were ordinary, she wouldn't feel like she needs to protect me as much. And Mom and Dad don't see me as ordinary, either. They see me as extraordinary. I think the only person in the world who realizes how ordinary I am is me.

My name is August, by the way. I won't describe what I look like. Whatever you're thinking, it's probably worse.

Basic reading skills

1   List four ordinary things that August says he does.

2   Why does August say he's not an ordinary ten-year-old kid?

3   If August had a magic lamp, what would he wish for?

4   What is the name of August's sister?

5   How do August's family act towards him? Explain any differences in the way they behave.

6   What impression do you get of August from this opening? Use a spider diagram to collect all the information you can about him from the text.

Advanced reading skills

1   In a first-person narrative, narrative voice is the voice of the character telling the story. The **tone** of voice they use can reflect their attitude towards their situation and the events of the story. Which of the words below do you think best describe the narrative voice in this extract? Explain your choice.

hopeful

conversational   sad   troubled

matter-of-fact

Key term

tone a manner of expression in speech or writing

2   In the last paragraph, August tells the reader, 'I won't describe what I look like. Whatever you're thinking, it's probably worse.' Why do you think R. J. Palacio has decided not to describe what August looks like?

3   Describe August in your own words. You should refer to details from the opening to support the points you make.

4   Choose the statement below that you most agree with and complete it in your own words.

I think this is an effective opening because...

I don't think this is an effective opening because...

6.2 *The Invisible Man* by H.G. Wells, 1897

The following text is the opening of a novel called *The Invisible Man* by H. G. Wells which is set towards the end of the 19th century. As you read, think about what you learn about who or what the novel is about.

Source text 6.2

WORD BANK

Bramblehurst railway station a railway station in East Sussex, England

portmanteau a type of travelling bag, usually made of stiff leather

Coach and Horses the name of an inn, a countryside pub offering accommodation

sovereigns gold coins used in Britain in the 19th century, worth one pound

quarters room, lodging

Iping a village in East Sussex, England

haggler someone who tries to bargain over the cost of something

good fortune good luck

lymphatic old-fashioned term meaning sluggish or slow-moving

brisked quickened, hurried

éclat style, brilliant display

The stranger came early in February, one wintry day, through a biting wind and a driving snow, the last snowfall of the year, over the down, walking from **Bramblehurst railway station** and carrying a little black **portmanteau** in his thickly gloved hand. He was wrapped up from head to foot, and the brim of his soft felt hat hid every inch of his face but the shiny tip of his nose; the snow had piled itself against his shoulders and chest, and added a white crest to the burden he carried. He staggered into the **Coach and Horses** more dead than alive, and flung his portmanteau down. 'A fire,' he cried, 'in the name of human charity! A room and a fire!' He stamped and shook the snow from off himself in the bar, and followed Mrs Hall into her guest parlour to strike his bargain. And with that much introduction, that and a couple of **sovereigns** flung upon the table, he took up his **quarters** in the inn.

Mrs Hall lit the fire and left him there while she went to prepare him a meal with her own hands. A guest to stop at **Iping** in the winter-time was an unheard-of piece of luck, let alone a guest who was no **'haggler'**, and she was resolved to show herself worthy of her **good fortune**.

As soon as the bacon was well under way, and Millie, her **lymphatic** aid, had been **brisked** up a bit by a few deftly chosen expressions of contempt, she carried the cloth, plates and glasses into the parlour and began to lay them with the utmost ***éclat***. Although the fire was burning up briskly, she was surprised to see that her visitor still wore his hat and coat, standing with his back to her and staring out of the window at the falling snow in the yard.

His gloved hands were clasped behind him, and he seemed to be lost in thought. She noticed that the melted snow that still sprinkled his shoulders dripped upon her carpet.

'Can I take your hat and coat, sir,' she said, 'and give them a good dry in the kitchen?'

'No,' he said without turning.

She was not sure she had heard him, and was about to repeat her question.

He turned his head and looked at her over his shoulder. 'I prefer to keep them on,' he said with emphasis, and she noticed that he wore big

WORD BANK

sidelights side-coverings worn on old-fashioned spectacles

staccato a series of short, sharp sounds or actions

stateliness a formal, dignified and elegant manner

rapped knocked

serviette a table napkin

blue spectacles with **sidelights**, and had a bushy side-whisker over his coat-collar that completely hid his cheeks and face.

'Very well, sir,' she said. 'As you like. In a bit the room will be warmer.'

He made no answer, and had turned his face away from her again; and Mrs Hall, feeling that her conversational advances were ill-timed, laid the rest of the table things in a quick **staccato** manner, and whisked out of the room. When she returned he was still standing there like a man of stone, his back hunched, his collar turned up, his dripping hat-brim turned down, hiding his face and ears completely. She put down the eggs and bacon with considerable emphasis, and called rather than said to him, 'Your lunch is served, sir.'

'Thank you,' he said at the same time, and did not stir until she was closing the door. Then he swung round and approached the table.

As she went behind the bar to the kitchen she heard a sound repeated at regular intervals. Chirk, chirk, chirk, it went, the sound of a spoon being rapidly whisked round a basin. 'That girl!' she said. 'There! I clean forgot it. It's her being so long!' And while she herself finished mixing the mustard, she gave Millie a few verbal stabs for her excessive slowness. She had cooked the ham and eggs, laid the table, and done everything, while Millie (help indeed!) had only succeeded in delaying the mustard. And him a new guest and wanting to stay! Then she filled the mustard pot, and, putting it with a certain **stateliness** upon a gold and black tea-tray, carried it into the parlour.

She **rapped** and entered promptly. As she did so her visitor moved quickly, so that she got but a glimpse of a white object disappearing behind the table. It would seem he was picking something from the floor. She rapped down the mustard pot on the table, and then she noticed the overcoat and hat had been taken off and put over a chair in front of the fire. A pair of wet boots threatened rust to her steel fender. She went to these things resolutely. 'I suppose I may have them to dry now,' she said in a voice that brooked no denial.

'Leave the hat,' said her visitor in a muffled voice, and turning she saw he had raised his head and was sitting and looking at her.

For a moment she stood gaping at him, too surprised to speak.

He held a white cloth – it was a **serviette** he had brought with him – over the lower part of his face, so that his mouth and jaws were completely hidden, and that was the reason of his muffled voice.

But it was not that which startled Mrs Hall. It was the fact that all his forehead above his blue glasses was covered by a white bandage, and that another covered his ears, leaving not a scrap of his face exposed excepting only his pink, peaked nose. It was bright pink, and shiny just as it had been at first. He wore a dark-brown velvet jacket with a high black linen-lined collar turned up about his neck. The thick black hair, escaping as it could below and between the cross bandages, projected in curious tails and horns, giving him the strangest appearance conceivable. This muffled and bandaged head was so unlike what she had anticipated, that for a moment she was rigid.

He did not remove the serviette, but remained holding it, as she saw now, with a brown gloved hand, and regarding her with his inscrutable blue glasses. 'Leave the hat,' he said, speaking very distinctly through the white cloth.

AVANT TOUT, DIT KEMP,

JE VOUDRAIS BIEN.

EN SAVOIR UN PEU PLUS LONG

SUR VOTRE INVISIBILITÉ.

Basic reading skills

1   Look again at the opening paragraph. What do you learn about the setting from this?

2   What does the stranger do when he first arrives at the Coach and Horses?

3   Why does Mrs Hall think the stranger's arrival is a piece of 'good fortune'?

4   Why does Mrs Hall return to the stranger's room?

5   As she sets the table, what surprises Mrs Hall about the stranger's appearance?

6   How does Mrs Hall react when she sees the stranger for the final time? What does this suggest about her feelings towards him?

Advanced reading skills

1   Compare the openings of *Wonder* and *The Invisible Man*. Copy and complete a table like the one below to collect your ideas.

Feature	*Wonder*	*The Invisible Man*
Narrative viewpoint and voice		
Characterization of the protagonist (the presentation of August or the stranger through thoughts, dialogue and actions)		
Mood (the tone or atmosphere conveyed)		
Theme (a subject or idea that recurs frequently in the work)		

2   Copy and complete the following statements in your own words.

> I think August in *Wonder* and the stranger in *The Invisible Man* are similar because...

> I think August in *Wonder* and the stranger in *The Invisible Man* are different because...

3   Which of these two openings most make you want to read on? Give reasons for your choice and why you preferred it.

6.3 *The Day of the Triffids* by John Wyndham, 1951

The following text is the opening of *The Day of the Triffids*, a science-fiction novel which was first published in 1951. As you read, think about how the writer makes you want to read on.

Source text 6.3

WORD BANK

misgave felt doubt or slight fear

objective not influenced by personal feelings or opinions

awry wrong, not according to plan

wreathed to wind something round

peevish irritable or bad-tempered

what in thunder an exclamation similar to 'What on earth'

matron a woman in charge of nursing staff in a hospital

latch work

hitherto until now

When a day that you happen to know is Wednesday starts off by sounding like Sunday, there is something seriously wrong somewhere.

I felt that from the moment I woke. And yet, when I started functioning a little more sharply, I **misgave**. After all, the odds were that it was I who was wrong, and not everyone else – though I did not see how that could be. I went on waiting, tinged with doubt. But presently I had my first bit of **objective** evidence – a distant clock struck what sounded to me just like eight. I listened hard and suspiciously. Soon another clock began, on a loud, decisive note. In a leisurely fashion it gave an indisputable eight. Then I *knew* things were **awry**.

The way I came to miss the end of the world – well, the end of the world I had known for close on thirty years – was sheer accident: like a lot of survival, when you come to think of it. In the nature of things a good many somebodies are always in hospital, and the law of averages had picked on me to be one of them a week or so before. It might just as easily have been the week before that – in which case I'd not be writing now: I'd not be here at all. But chance played it not only that I should be in hospital at that particular time, but that my eyes, and indeed my whole head, should be **wreathed** in bandages – and that's why I have to be grateful to whoever orders these averages. At the time, however, I was only **peevish**, wondering **what in thunder** went on, for I had been in the place long enough to know that, next to the **matron**, the clock is the most sacred thing in a hospital.

Without a clock the place simply couldn't **latch**. Each second there's someone consulting it on births, deaths, doses, meals, lights, talking, working, sleeping, resting, visiting, dressing, washing – and **hitherto** it had decreed that someone should begin to wash and tidy me up at exactly three minutes after 7 a.m. That was one of the best reasons I had for appreciating a private room. In a public ward the messy proceeding would have taken place a whole unnecessary hour earlier. But here, today, clocks of varying reliability were continuing to strike eight in all directions – and still nobody had shown up.

Basic reading skills

1 Where is the opening of this novel set?

2 Re-read the first two paragraphs. Which of the following words would you use to describe the narrator's mood in this section of the extract? Explain your choice.

nervous   terrified   excited   anxious   calm   depressed

3 What is the 'first bit of objective evidence' the narrator notices that justifies his mood?

4 How old is the narrator?

5 What part of the narrator's body is in bandages?

6 Re-read the final paragraph. List four reasons the narrator gives why people need to consult a clock in a hospital.

7 What time should the narrator have been woken at and why?

Advanced reading skills

1 Look again at the opening line. How effectively does this hook a reader's interest?

2 How does the writer create a sense of the narrator's unease? Think about the language used and the descriptive details included.

3 Pick out any details from the extract that suggest this is the opening of a science-fiction novel. Give reasons for your choices.

4a Most novels are written in the past tense, as is this opening from *The Day of the Triffids*. Rewrite the second paragraph in the present tense.

4b Compare your rewritten paragraph with the original version. Which do you prefer and why?

5 In one sentence, predict what you think will happen next in the story.

Extended reading

How effective do you think this extract is as the opening of a science-fiction novel? Use some or all of these questions to structure your response:

- What happens in the text and how does this engage the reader's interest?

- How does the author establish the narrator and make the reader interested in him?

- How does the author create a sense of the setting?

- Did the opening make you want to continue reading the novel? Why or why not?

- Does the opening meet your expectations of a science-fiction novel? Explain why or why not.

Extended writing

Write the opening of a novel. You could use one of the following titles for inspiration or base your story on your own idea.

An unexpected event

Behind the mask

The day everything changed

Think about how you can draw on different techniques from the three texts you have read in this section. In your story you should:

- choose a narrative viewpoint (for example, first or third person)

- begin the narrative with an event or statement that captures the reader's interest

- introduce and establish characters and setting

- use language to create the appropriate mood in your writing

- structure your writing in a way that draws the reader into the story.

Remember to check the spelling, punctuation and grammar of your writing.

 **Early bird**

How many different ways can you write the following sentence?

The girl swung, high above the ground, her legs dangling into empty air.

You can reorder, expand or omit details, changing punctuation if required, but you must keep the meaning of the sentence the same. Then choose the version of the sentence you think would make the most effective opening for a story.

Source texts table

Text	Date
7.1 *After Tomorrow* by Gillian Cross	2013
7.2 'A Piece of Cake' by Roald Dahl	1942
7.3 *The Sign of Four* by Arthur Conan Doyle	1890

Big picture

If you look up the word 'action' in the dictionary, this is one of the definitions you will find: 'an action is something someone does'. In fiction, these actions can be large or small, from the murder of a leading character in a detective thriller to the loss of a note in a romance story. The action of the story is the events that keep readers turning the pages to find out what happens next. What are the most memorable scenes you can remember from the stories you have read? In this section you'll read extracts from novels and a short story from the 19th, 20th and 21st centuries, and explore how their authors use action to drive the narrative.

Skills

- Understand the meaning of a text
- Make inferences and refer to evidence in the text
- Explore how writers use language and structure to convey action
- Compare texts
- Use techniques explored in reading to convey character in your own writing

Before reading

1. 'Writers need to think about the focus of a scene and cut straight to the action. Otherwise readers will get bored.'

   Do you agree or disagree with the above statement? Discuss whether you think this is useful advice for writers.

2. 'Action' is also a genre of story, typically used for films which include violence, chases and physical danger. Create your own list of ingredients for an action story.

3. Think about a story you know well and discuss whether you think it belongs to the action genre.

7.1 *After Tomorrow* by Gillian Cross, 2013

The following extract is taken from the novel *After Tomorrow* by Gillian Cross. This novel is set in a near-future Britain where money is worthless and armed robbers roam the streets. Here, Matt describes how he is sitting down for tea with his mother, younger brother Taco and stepfather Justin, when masked raiders break into their home. As you read, think about the action of the scene and how this makes you feel as a reader.

Source text 7.1

So it was a normal, dull evening. And then suddenly, without any warning—

CRASH!!!

The back door burst open, splintering away from its hinges, and two men in balaclavas leapt into the kitchen. They were yelling at the tops of their voices.

'OK! Nobody move! Hands on the table!'

'Shut your mouths!'

They were both holding big, heavy wrenches, swinging them round like weapons. Justin began to stand up—and then sank slowly back into his chair. He looked stupid, but it made sense.

If a wrench like that smashed into your skull, it wouldn't just give you a bruise.

The men didn't hesitate. One of them grabbed Taco and yanked him backwards in his chair, holding the wrench over his face. The other one ripped open the cupboard doors, one after another—until he found the food cupboard.

He started emptying it straight away, scooping out pasta and beans and cereal—all the food Mum had stashed away so carefully. He loaded it all into trolley bags, cramming them full.

'Don't take *everything*,' Justin bleated, when he opened the freezer. 'We've got children to feed.'

'It's your kids or ours, mate,' said the other man.

He swung his wrench high in the air over Taco's head and looked sideways at Justin. Taco's spoon shook, spilling swede back on to the plate, and his eyes opened wide and white.

79

Justin opened his mouth to argue—and then shut it again, without saying anything.

'That's better,' the man said grimly. 'We don't want any trouble.'

All our frozen food went into the next couple of bags. Beans. Beetroot. Carrots. Apple. Our precious sausages and bacon and the bony bits of lamb for stewing. For a second there was no sound except the thump of frozen meat dropping into the bag. Then Mum put an arm around Taco's shoulders and started whispering in his ear.

The wrench swung towards her sharply. She glanced up at it and stopped talking, but she didn't move her arm.

In fifteen minutes, all the cupboards were bare. The fridge and the freezer were standing empty, with their doors wide open and the ice slowly starting to melt. The man with the bags took them out into the hall and lined them up by the front door. Then he went out—leaving the other one to guard us.

That was our chance! We should have jumped him then. Justin could have knocked him sideways **CRUNCH! THUMP!** and I could have sat on his head while Mum grabbed the wrench. Then we'd have attacked the other man when he came back and **BANG! ZAP!! POW!!!** we would have been in charge. We'd have made them put all our food back and then tied them up and called the police.

My dad would have done that. He would have picked up those weedy little raiders and smashed their heads together. But Justin didn't move. Not an inch. He went on sitting meekly at the table, watching the wrench that was aimed at Mum's head.

Basic reading skills

1 What three instructions do the masked raiders give when they break into the kitchen?

2 What weapons are the raiders armed with?

3 How does the writer suggest Taco's fear? Find a phrase or sentence in the text that supports your explanation.

4 One of the raiders says, 'It's your kids or ours, mate.' Explain what you think the raider means by this.

5 Create a storyboard to show the action of this scene. Label each frame of your storyboard with a sentence describing the key event shown.

Advanced reading skills

1 The verbs a writer chooses can influence the way a reader visualizes the action depicted. How does the writer's choice of verbs influence the way you visualize the following characters?

- The armed raiders

- Justin

2 Read what this student says about the text:

In the action of this scene, the threat of violence is never far from the surface.

a Do you agree with this statement? Copy and complete the table below by picking out quotations where violence is either explicitly shown or implied. Some examples have been given.

Explicit violence	Implicit violence
'The back door burst open, splintering away from its hinges'	'The wrench swung towards her sharply'

b Choose one quotation from each column of the above table and explore the effects it creates. Then explain which quotation you find most effective and why.

3 What impression do you get of Matt's attitude towards Justin? Explore how the following help to build this impression:

- Justin's dialogue and the way he speaks

- Justin's reactions to the events of the scene

- the way Matt describes Justin.

4 Re-read the paragraph beginning 'That was our chance!'

a How realistic do you think Matt's plan is?

b Identify the writer's use of onomatopoeia here and explain what effect this has on the way the action is described.

5 This scene is taken from the opening of the novel. Complete the following statement:

> I think the writer has chosen to begin the novel with this scene because...

7.2 'A Piece of Cake' by Roald Dahl,1942

The following extract is taken from Roald Dahl's short story 'A Piece of Cake' which takes place during the Second World War. Here, a pilot is flying his plane low over the Libyan desert as he searches for his destination. As you read, think about how the action of the crash is conveyed and how this makes you feel as a reader.

Source text 7.2

WORD BANK

telegraph system a communications system for sending messages by using electrical current along wires or by radio

I know only that there was trouble, lots and lots of trouble, and I know that we had turned round and were coming back when the trouble got worse. The biggest trouble of all was that I was too low to bail out, and it is from that point on that my memory comes back to me. I remember the dipping of the nose of the aircraft and I remember looking down the nose of the machine at the ground and seeing a little clump of camel-thorn growing there all by itself. I remember seeing some rocks lying in the sand beside the camel-thorn, and the camel-thorn and the sand and the rocks leapt out of the ground and came to me. I remember that very clearly.

Then there was a small gap of not-remembering. It might have been one second or it might have been thirty; I do not know. I have an idea that it was very short, a second perhaps, and next I heard a *crumph* on the right as the starboard wing tank caught fire, then another *crumph* on the left as the port tank did the same. To me that was not significant, and for a while I sat still, feeling comfortable, but a little drowsy. I couldn't see with my eyes, but that was not significant either. There was nothing to worry about. Nothing at all. Not until I felt the hotness around my legs. At first it was only a warmness and that was all right too, but all at once it was a hotness, a very stinging scorching hotness up and down the sides of each leg.

I knew that the hotness was unpleasant, but that was all I knew. I disliked it, so I curled my legs up under the seat and waited. I think there was something wrong with the **telegraph system** between the body and the brain. It did not seem to be working very well. Somehow it was a bit slow in telling the brain all about it and in asking for instructions. But I believe a message eventually got through, saying, 'Down here there is a great hotness. What shall we do? (Signed) Left Leg and Right Leg.' For a long time there was no reply. The brain was figuring the matter out.

Then slowly, word by word, the answer was tapped over the wires. 'The – plane – is – burning. Get – out – repeat – get – out – get – out.' The order was relayed to the whole system, to all the muscles in the legs, arms and body, and the muscles went to work. They tried their

best; they pushed a little and pulled a little, and they strained greatly, but it wasn't any good. Up went another telegram. 'Can't get out. Something holding us in.' The answer to this one took even longer in arriving, so I just sat there waiting for it to come, and all the time the hotness increased. Something was holding me down and it was up to the brain to find out what it was. Was it giants' hands pressing on my shoulders, or heavy stones or houses or steamrollers or filing cabinets or gravity or was it ropes? Wait a minute. Ropes – ropes. The message was beginning to come through. It came very slowly. 'Your – straps. Undo – your – straps.' My arms received the message and went to work. They tugged at the straps, but they wouldn't undo. They tugged again and again, a little feebly, but as hard as they could, and it wasn't any use. Back went the message, 'How do we undo the straps?'

This time I think that I sat there for three or four minutes waiting for the answer. It wasn't any use hurrying or getting impatient. That was the one thing of which I was sure. But what a long time it was all taking. I said aloud, 'Bugger it. I'm going to be burnt. I'm...' but I was interrupted. The answer was coming – no, it wasn't – yes, it was, it was slowly coming through. 'Pull – out – the – quick – release – pin – you – bloody – fool – and – hurry.'

Out came the pin and the straps were loosed. Now, let's get out. Let's get out, let's get out. But I couldn't do it. I simply lift myself out of the cockpit. Arms and legs tried their best but it wasn't any use. A last desperate message was flashed upwards and this time it was marked 'Urgent'.

'Something else is holding us down,' it said. 'Something else, something else, something heavy.'

Still the arms and legs did not fight. They seemed to know instinctively that there was no point in using up their strength. They stayed quiet and waited for the answer, and oh what a time it took. Twenty, thirty, forty hot seconds. None of them really white hot yet, no sizzling of flesh or smell of burning meat, but that would come any moment now, because those old **Gladiators** aren't made of stressed steel like a **Hurricane** or a **Spit**. They have taut canvas wings, covered with magnificently inflammable dope, and underneath there are hundreds of small thin sticks, the kind you put under the logs for kindling, only these are drier and thinner. If a clever man said, 'I am going to build a big thing that will burn better and quicker than anything else in the world,' and if he applied himself diligently to his task, he would probably finish up by building something very like a Gladiator. I sat still waiting.

WORD BANK

Gladiator a biplane

Hurricane a fighter aircraft

Spit Spitfire, a fighter aircraft

> Then suddenly the reply, beautiful in its briefness, but at the same time explaining everything. 'Your – parachute – turn – the – buckle.'
>
> I turned the buckle, released the parachute harness and with some effort hoisted myself up and tumbled over the side of the cockpit. Something seemed to be burning, so I rolled about a bit in the sand, then crawled away from the fire on all fours and lay down.
>
> I heard some of my machine-gun ammunition going off in the heat and I heard some of the bullets thumping into the sand near by. I did not worry about them; I merely heard them.
>
> Things were beginning to hurt.

Basic reading skills

1   Re-read the opening paragraph. Why can't the narrator bail out of his plane?

2   On what part of his body does the narrator first feel the heat of the fire?

3   'I think there was something wrong with the telegraph system between the body and the brain.' Using your own words, explain what the problem is.

4   Which of the following things keeps the narrator from getting out of his seat?

- Ropes

- Gravity

- Straps

- Heavy stones

5   When the narrator escapes from the burning plane, what other danger does he face?

Advanced reading skills

1   Re-read the opening paragraph. What effect does the writer's use of repetition create here?

2   Re-read the second paragraph. How does the way this paragraph is structured help to build a sense of tension? Think about:

- what the writer focuses your attention on at the start of the paragraph

- the sequence of events described in the paragraph and how the narrator reacts to these

- the writer's use of **adverbials of time** and the effects these create

- what the writer focuses your attention on at the end of the paragraph.

Key term

adverbial of time a word or phrase that is used as an adverb to indicate when something happened, for how long or the frequency of an action

3a Copy and complete the following table to identify how the writer uses different senses to describe the narrator's experience.

Hearing	Smell	Sight	Touch
'I heard a... *crumph* on the left as the port tank did the same'			

3b Choose the sensory detail that you find most effective and explain how it helps you to imagine the action of the scene.

4 How does the writer's use of language help to build tension throughout the extract? In your answer you should comment on:

- the writer's choices of vocabulary and descriptive details

- the extended metaphor of the 'telegraph system' and the effects this creates

- the sentence forms used and the effects these create.

5 Read what this student says about the action in this extract:

The action in this scene mostly takes place inside the narrator's mind.

Explain what you think the student means and then say whether you agree or disagree with their statement. Justify your answer with reference to the text.

7.3 *The Sign of Four* by Arthur Conan Doyle, 1890

The following text is taken from the novel *The Sign of Four* by Arthur Conan Doyle. In this novel, Sherlock Holmes and Dr Watson are investigating a case involving missing treasure. Here, accompanied by Mary Morstan and Thaddeus Sholto, they call on Thaddeus's twin brother Bartholomew, who they believe has the treasure, but he doesn't answer the door. As you read, think about how the action of the scene unfolds.

Source text 7.3

Holmes advanced along it in the same slow and methodical way, while we kept close at his heels, with our long black shadows streaming backward down the corridor. The third door was that which we were seeking. Holmes knocked without receiving any answer, and then tried to turn the handle and force it open. It was locked on the inside, however, and by a broad and powerful bolt, as we could see when we set our lamp up against it. The key being turned, however, the hole was not entirely closed. Sherlock Holmes bent down to it, and instantly rose again with a sharp intaking of the breath.

'There is something devilish in this, Watson,' said he, more moved than I had ever before seen him. 'What do you make of it?'

I stooped to the hole, and **recoiled** in horror. Moonlight was streaming into the room, and it was bright with a vague and shifty radiance. Looking straight at me, and suspended, as it were, in the air, for all beneath was in shadow, there hung a face—the very face of our companion Thaddeus. There was the same high, shining head, the same circular bristle of red hair, the same bloodless **countenance**. The features were set, however, in a horrible smile, a fixed and unnatural grin, which in that still and moonlit room was more jarring to the nerves than any scowl or contortion. So like was the face to that of our little friend that I looked round at him to make sure that he was indeed with us. Then I recalled to mind that he had mentioned to us that his brother and he were twins.

'This is terrible!' I said to Holmes. 'What is to be done?'

'The door must come down,' he answered, and, springing against it, he put all his weight upon the lock.

It creaked and groaned, but did not yield. Together we flung ourselves upon it once more, and this time it gave way with a sudden snap, and we found ourselves within Bartholomew Sholto's chamber.

It appeared to have been fitted up as a chemical laboratory. A double line of glass-stoppered bottles was drawn up upon the wall opposite the door, and the table was littered over with Bunsen burners, test-tubes, and **retorts**. In the corners stood **carboys** of acid in wicker baskets.

WORD BANK

recoiled moved back suddenly in shock or disgust

countenance a person's face

retorts glass vessels used for distilling liquids

carboys large, globe-shaped glass bottles with narrow necks, typically used for storing acid

One of these appeared to leak or to have been broken, for a stream of dark-coloured liquid had trickled out from it, and the air was heavy with a peculiarly pungent, tar-like odour. A set of steps stood at one side of the room, in the midst of a litter of lath and plaster, and above them there was an opening in the ceiling large enough for a man to pass through. At the foot of the steps a long coil of rope was thrown carelessly together.

By the table, in a wooden armchair, the master of the house was seated all in a heap, with his head sunk upon his left shoulder, and that ghastly, **inscrutable** smile upon his face. He was stiff and cold, and had clearly been dead many hours. It seemed to me that not only his features but all his limbs were twisted and turned in the most fantastic fashion. By his hand upon the table there lay a peculiar instrument—a brown, close-grained stick, with a stone head like a hammer, rudely lashed on with coarse twine. Beside it was a torn sheet of notepaper with some words scrawled upon it. Holmes glanced at it, and then handed it to me.

'You see,' he said, with a significant raising of the eyebrows. In the light of the lantern I read, with a thrill of horror, 'The sign of the four.'

'In God's name, what does it all mean?' I asked.

'It means murder,' said he, stooping over the dead man. 'Ah, I expected it. Look here!'

He pointed to what looked like a long dark thorn stuck in the skin just above the ear.

'It looks like a thorn,' said I.

'It is a thorn. You may pick it out. But be careful, for it is poisoned.'

I took it up between my finger and thumb. It came away from the skin so readily that hardly any mark was left behind. One tiny speck of blood showed where the puncture had been.

'This is all an **insoluble** mystery to me,' said I. 'It grows darker instead of clearer.'

'On the contrary,' he answered, 'it clears every instant. I only require a few missing links to have an entirely connected case.'

WORD BANK

inscrutable mysterious, impossible to interpret

insoluble impossible to solve

Basic reading skills

1 Re-read the first paragraph.

   a Select a word or phrase that best describes how Sherlock Holmes walks down the corridor.

   b Why can't Sherlock Holmes open the third door?

   c How does Sherlock Holmes see inside the room?

2 Re-read the paragraph beginning 'I stooped to the hole and recoiled in horror.' List three physical details about the man inside the room.

3 Which two details lead Dr Watson to state the man 'had clearly been dead many hours'?

4 How has the man died? Select the correct reason from the list below.

- He has been hung from a rope.

- He has been poisoned.

- He has been struck with a hammer.

- He has fallen through a hole in the ceiling.

5a Select one piece of evidence that shows Dr Watson is finding it difficult to solve the case.

5b Select one piece of evidence that shows that Sherlock Holmes is close to solving the case.

Advanced reading skills

1 'For every action there should be a reaction.' Compare the ways Sherlock Holmes and Dr Watson react to their first view of the room's interior. What does this reveal about their characters?

2 Re-read from the paragraph beginning '"The door must come down," he answered.' What does the writer's choice of verbs suggest about how they break into the room?

3a Pick an adjective that best describes the mood of this extract from the list below.

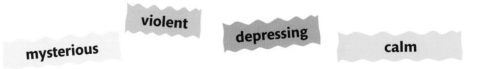

sinister   mysterious   violent   depressing   calm

3b Select a quotation and explain how you think it helps to create this mood.

4   The extract from *After Tomorrow* shows a violent robbery taking place, while the extract from *The Sign of Four* shows the aftermath of a murder. Compare the ways these two writers use language to convey the action of these scenes. You should comment on:

- the adverbs and adjectives chosen to describe the action

- the writers' use of dialogue

- the writers' choices of vocabulary and descriptive details

- the writers' choices of sentence types and forms.

Extended reading

Narrative pace is the speed at which a story is told. Analyse the narrative pace of *one* of the extracts you have read in this section. In your analysis, you should explore:

- the length of the sentences and paragraphs and the impact these have on the narrative pace

- the balance between action and description in the extract and what effect this creates

- how fast the action moves and how quickly the reader is provided with information.

Extended writing

Look again at the extract from *After Tomorrow*. Write a scene where the masked raiders break into Matt's home again, but this time the family fight back. As you write, think about:

- how you can use vocabulary, descriptive details and figurative language to convey the action of the scene

- how your choice of sentence forms and paragraph lengths can influence the pace of the narrative

- the structure of your writing and the way you can guide the reader's eye within and between paragraphs by focusing on specific details.

Remember to check the spelling, punctuation and grammar of your writing.

Early bird

Try to create five surprising sentences using the verb 'explodes'. One has been done for you.

The teardrop explodes.

Source texts table

Text	Date
8.1 *The London Eye Mystery* by Siobhan Dowd	2007
8.2 *The Prime of Miss Jean Brodie* by Muriel Spark	1961
8.3 *Pride and Prejudice* by Jane Austen	1813

Big picture

'Hey, there! Want to know how dialogue works?' Dialogue is what the characters in a story say. This can be used to reveal a character's thoughts, emotions and also provide information that moves the plot of the story forward. Can you think of a line of dialogue that has stayed with you after you have closed the pages of a favourite book? In this section, you'll read extracts from novels written in the 19th, 20th and 21st centuries and explore the different effects the use of dialogue can create.

Skills

- Understand the meaning of a text

- Make inferences and refer to evidence in the text

- Explore how dialogue is used to convey character and create mood

- Draw on the techniques studied to write convincing dialogue

Before reading

1   Dialogue tags are verbs used to indicate which character is speaking. For example:

'Where are you?' *asked* Dan.

'I'm over here,' Penelope *replied*.

'That's the safest place,' *said* the man.

Match the following dialogue tags to the emotion you think they convey.

Dialogue tag		Emotion
sobbed		disappointment
giggled		aggression
hissed		happiness
whined		satisfaction
purred		sadness

2   'Most of the time "said" is the only verb that should be used to indicate who is speaking in a story.'

Do you agree or disagree with this statement? Give reasons and try to find examples of dialogue from the extracts in this book to support your point of view.

8.1 *The London Eye Mystery* by Siobhan Dowd, 2007

The following extract is taken from *The London Eye Mystery*, a novel by Siobhan Dowd. In this story, Ted, his older sister Kat and their cousin Salim go to the London Eye, a giant Ferris wheel on the South Bank of the River Thames in London. Accepting a ticket from a stranger, Salim boards one of the pods to take a ride on the London Eye, but when the wheel completes its journey round, Salim is nowhere to be seen. Here, Ted and Kat go to find their mother and Aunt Gloria, who is Salim's mother, to tell them what has happened.

Source text 8.1

We walked over to where Mum and Aunt Gloria were having coffee.

'Let's lie,' hissed Kat. 'About taking that ticket from a stranger.' She grabbed me by the wrist so hard it hurt.

'Lie,' I repeated. 'Hrumm. Lie.'

'We could say that Salim got lost in the crowds, that he—' She let my wrist go. 'Oh, forget it,' she said. 'I know telling a lie with you is useless. And stop doing that duck-that's-forgotten-how-to-quack look!'

We reached the table where Aunt Gloria and Mum sat talking up another storm. We stood by them in silence. A pounding started up in my ears, as if my blood pressure had shot up above normal, which is what Mum says happens to her when Kat drives her distracted.

'There you are,' Aunt Gloria said. 'Have you got the tickets?'

Kat waited for me to say something.

I waited for Kat to say something.

'Where's Salim?' asked Mum. 'Not still in the queue?'

'Hrumm,' I said. 'No.'

Mum looked as if Salim might be behind us. 'Where then?'

'We don't know!' Kat blurted. 'This man – he came up and offered us a ticket. For free. He'd bought it and then decided he couldn't face the ride.'

'He had claustrophobia,' I said.

'That's right. And the queue was terrible. So we took the ticket. And gave it to Salim. And Salim went up on his own. And he didn't come down.'

Aunt Gloria shaded her eyes and looked up. 'So he's up there somewhere,' she said, smiling.

Kat had a hand to her mouth and her fingers were wriggling like worms. I'd never seen her act like this before. 'No,' she said. 'He went up ages ago. Ted and I tracked his pod. But when it came down – he wasn't on it.'

Mum's face scrunched up, which meant she was a) puzzled or b) cross or c) both. 'What on earth do you mean, he wasn't on it?'

'He went up, Mum,' I repeated. 'But he didn't come down.' My hand flapped and Mum's mouth went round like an O. 'He defied the law of gravity, Mum. He went up but he didn't come down. Which means Newton got it wrong. Hrumm.'

Mum looked more cross than puzzled by now. But Aunt Gloria's face remained smooth like paper without a crease. 'Bet I know what happened,' she said, smiling.

'What?' we all said.

'He probably went round one more time.'

The simplicity of this solution struck Kat and me at once.

'That's it. He just stayed on,' said Kat.

I looked at my watch. 'In which case he'll land at twelve thirty-two.'

We went back to the Eye, this time with Mum. Aunt Gloria said she would stay where she was, because Salim would know where to find her if we missed him.

We watched several pods open and close, but no Salim. 12.32 came and went. No Salim.

Basic reading skills

1 Re-read the opening four paragraphs.

   a What does Kat want to tell Mum and Aunt Gloria about what has happened to Salim?

   b What action does Kat perform that suggests she wants Ted to do as she says?

   c What word does Ted repeat? What does this suggest he thinks about Kat's suggestion?

   d Why does she change her mind about what they should say to Mum and Aunt Gloria?

2 The narrator says his mum and Aunt Gloria are 'sat talking up another storm'. Using your own words, explain what this phrase suggests.

3 Why does Ted say the man gave them a free ticket for the London Eye?

4 'Mum's face scrunched up' but 'Aunt Gloria's face remained smooth like paper without a crease'. Explain what this contrast suggests about their different emotions.

5 Where does Aunt Gloria think Salim is?

Advanced reading skills

1   The way people speak reflects who they are. What different impressions do you get of Ted and Kat from their dialogue in this extract? You should comment on:

   ■   what each character says and how they say it

   ■   the vocabulary each character uses and the impression this creates

   ■   the sentence forms each character uses and the effects these create.

2   Look at Mum's and Aunt Gloria's dialogue. Copy and complete the following sentences to explain how their reaction to Ted and Kat changes.

> When Mum says, 'What on earth do you mean, he wasn't on it?' this shows...

> When Aunt Gloria says, 'Bet I know what happened' this suggests...

3   Look at the following student's statement about the extract:

The dialogue adds to the tension of this scene.

   a   Explain whether you agree or disagree with this statement.

   b   Find the most tense line of dialogue and explain your choice.

4   This extract is written in the first person from Ted's perspective.

   a   Choose a word from the list below that you think best describes Ted's narrative voice.

worried
conversational
sensitive
thoughtful
determined
touching

   b   Give reasons for your choice.

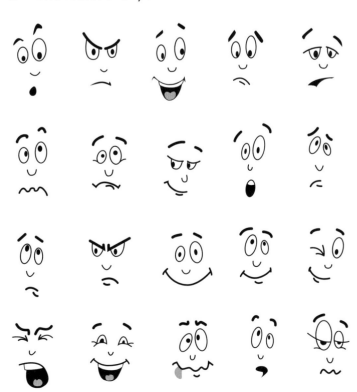

8.2 *The Prime of Miss Jean Brodie* by Muriel Spark, 1961

The following extract is taken from the novel *The Prime of Miss Jean Brodie* by Muriel Spark, which is set in an Edinburgh school in the 1930s. Miss Brodie is a teacher who has recently returned from holiday in Italy. Here, at the beginning of the school year, her classroom is visited by the headmistress, Miss Mackay.

Source text 8.2

'Good morning, sit down, girls,' said the headmistress who had entered in a hurry, leaving the door wide open.

Miss Brodie passed behind her with her head up, up, and shut the door with the utmost meaning.

'I have only just looked in,' said Miss Mackay, 'and I have to be off. Well, girls, this is the first day of the new session. Are we downhearted? No. You girls must work hard this year at every subject and pass your qualifying examination with flying colours. Next year you will be in the Senior school, remember. I hope you've all had a nice summer holiday, you all look nice and brown. I hope in due course of time to read your essays on how you spent them.'

When she had gone Miss Brodie looked hard at the door for a long time. A girl, not of her set, called Judith, giggled. Miss Brodie said to Judith, 'That will do.' She turned to the blackboard and rubbed out with her duster the long division sum she always kept on the blackboard in case of intrusions from outside during any arithmetic periods when Miss Brodie should happen not to be teaching arithmetic. When she had done this she turned back to the class and said, 'Are we downhearted no, are we downhearted no. As I was saying, **Mussolini** has performed feats of **magnitude** and unemployment is even farther abolished under him than it was last year. I shall be able to tell you a great deal this term. As you know, I don't believe in talking down to children, you are capable of grasping more than is generally appreciated by your elders. Education means a leading out, from *e*, out and *duco*, I lead. Qualifying examination or no qualifying examination, you will have the benefit of my experiences in Italy. In Rome I saw the **Forum** and I saw the **Colosseum** where the gladiators died and the slaves were thrown to the lions. A vulgar American remarked to me, "It looks like a mighty fine quarry." They talk nasally. Mary, what does to talk nasally mean?'

Mary did not know.

'Stupid as ever,' said Miss Brodie. 'Eunice?'

'Through your nose,' said Eunice.

WORD BANK

Mussolini Benito Mussolini, the fascist leader of Italy from 1922 to 1943

magnitude great importance

e Latin word meaning 'out'

duco Latin word meaning 'to lead'

Forum the public square surrounded by the ruins of important ancient government buildings in Rome

Colosseum an ancient Roman amphitheatre used for gladiatorial battles and public entertainments

'Answer in a complete sentence, please,' said Miss Brodie. 'This year I think you should all start answering in complete sentences, I must try to remember this rule. Your correct answer is "To talk nasally means to talk through one's nose". The American said, "It looks like a mighty fine quarry." Ah! It was there the gladiators fought. "Hail Caesar!" they cried. "These about to die salute thee!"'

Miss Brodie stood in her brown dress like a gladiator with raised arm and eyes flashing like a sword. 'Hail Caesar!' she cried again, turning radiantly to the window light, as if Caesar sat there. 'Who opened the window?' said Miss Brodie dropping her arm.

Nobody answered.

'Whoever has opened the window has opened it too wide,' said Miss Brodie. 'Six inches is perfectly adequate. More is vulgar. One should have an **innate** sense of these things. We ought to be doing history at the moment according to the time-table. Get out your history books and prop them up in your hands. I shall tell you a little more about Italy.'

WORD BANK

innate inborn or natural

Basic reading skills

1   Why does the headmistress say the girls need to work hard this year?

2   List two things Miss Brodie does that show her annoyance at the headmistress.

3   Why does Miss Brodie keep a long division sum on her blackboard?

4   Miss Brodie says, 'I don't believe in talking down to children, you are capable of grasping more than is generally appreciated by your elders.' Using your own words, explain what she means by this.

5a Choose an adjective from the list below that you think best describes Miss Brodie's personality.

rude   superior   strict   refined
mean   stern   polite

5b Select the line of Miss Brodie's dialogue that you think best suggests your chosen adjective. Explain your choice of quotation.

Advanced reading skills

1   Re-read the opening three paragraphs. What impression do you get of the headmistress from this section? Think about her actions and dialogue.

2   Which line of dialogue does Miss Brodie repeat? What is the effect of this repetition?

3   What impression do you get of Miss Brodie from this extract? Think about:

   ■ what she says and the way she says it

   ■ her actions and the way these are described

   ■ how the students respond to her.

4   Do you think Miss Brodie is a good or bad teacher? Justify your answer with evidence from the text.

8.3 *Pride and Prejudice* by Jane Austen, 1813

The following extract is taken from the opening to the novel *Pride and Prejudice* by Jane Austen, which was first published in 1813. At this time, one of the only ways a young woman could improve her fortunes was by marrying a wealthy husband. Here, Mrs Bennet informs Mr Bennet that the neighbouring manor of Netherfield Park has been rented by a young gentleman who Mrs Bennet hopes might be interested in marrying one of her five daughters. As you read the extract, think about the impression you get of Mr and Mrs Bennet from their dialogue.

Source text 8.3

WORD BANK

chaise and four a
carriage drawn by
four horses

Michaelmas a Christian
festival which
takes place on
29 September

design plan

'My dear Mr. Bennet,' said his lady to him one day, 'have you heard that Netherfield Park is let at last?'

Mr. Bennet replied that he had not.

'But it is,' returned she; 'for Mrs. Long has just been here, and she told me all about it.'

Mr. Bennet made no answer.

'Do not you want to know who has taken it?' cried his wife impatiently.

'*You* want to tell me, and I have no objection to hearing it.'

This was invitation enough.

'Why, my dear, you must know, Mrs. Long says that Netherfield is taken by a young man of large fortune from the north of England; that he came down on Monday in a **chaise and four** to see the place, and was so much delighted with it that he agreed with Mr. Morris immediately; that he is to take possession before **Michaelmas**, and some of his servants are to be in the house by the end of next week.'

'What is his name?'

'Bingley.'

'Is he married or single?'

'Oh! single, my dear, to be sure! A single man of large fortune; four or five thousand a year. What a fine thing for our girls!'

'How so? how can it affect them?'

'My dear Mr. Bennet,' replied his wife, 'how can you be so tiresome! You must know that I am thinking of his marrying one of them.'

'Is that his **design** in settling here?'

'Design! nonsense, how can you talk so! But it is very likely that he *may* fall in love with one of them, and therefore you must visit him as soon as he comes.'

'I see no occasion for that. You and the girls may go, or you may send them by themselves, which perhaps will be still better, for as you are as handsome as any of them, Mr. Bingley may like you the best of the party.'

'My dear, you flatter me. I certainly *have* had my share of beauty, but I do not pretend to be anything extraordinary now. When a woman has five grown up daughters, she ought to give over thinking of her own beauty.'

'In such cases, a woman has not often much beauty to think of.'

'But, my dear, you must indeed go and see Mr. Bingley when he comes into the neighbourhood.'

'It is more than I engage for, I assure you.'

'But consider your daughters. Only think what an establishment it would be for one of them. Sir William and Lady Lucas are determined to go, merely on that account, for in general you know they visit no new comers. Indeed you must go, for it will be impossible for *us* to visit him, if you do not.'

'You are over scrupulous, surely. I dare say Mr. Bingley will be very glad to see you; and I will send a few lines by you to assure him of my hearty consent to his marrying which ever he **chuses** of the girls; though I must throw in a good word for my little Lizzy.'

'I desire you will do no such thing. Lizzy is not a bit better than the others; and I am sure she is not half so handsome as Jane, nor half so good humoured as Lydia. But you are always giving *her* the preference.'

'They have none of them much to recommend them,' replied he; 'they are all silly and ignorant like other girls; but Lizzy has something more of quickness than her sisters.'

'Mr. Bennet, how can you abuse your own children in such a way? You take delight in **vexing** me. You have no compassion for my poor nerves.'

'You mistake me, my dear. I have a high respect for your nerves. They are my old friends. I have heard you mention them with consideration these last twenty years at least.'

'Ah! you do not know what I suffer.'

'But I hope you will get over it, and live to see many young men of four thousand a year come into the neighbourhood.'

'It will be no use to us, if twenty such should come since you will not visit them.'

'Depend upon it, my dear, that when there are twenty, I will visit them all.'

WORD BANK

chuses chooses

vexing annoying

Basic reading skills

1   What is the name of the man who has rented Netherfield Park?

2   Why does Mrs Bennet call her husband 'tiresome'? Choose the correct answer from the list below.

- He doesn't listen to what she says.

- He doesn't understand why she is excited.

- He won't agree to visit Mr Bingley.

- He doesn't know that Netherfield Park has been let.

3 Why does Mrs Bennet want Mr Bennet to visit Mr Bingley as soon as he comes?

4 Which of his daughters does Mr Bennet prefer? Justify your choice with evidence from the text.

Advanced reading skills

1 *Pride and Prejudice* is set in the early 19th century. Pick out one example of dialogue that you think best indicates the time the story is set. Explain your choice.

2 Dialogue can reveal a character's attitudes and personality. Later in the chapter, Mrs Bennet is described as 'a woman of mean understanding, little information, and uncertain temper'.

Explain what you think this description means in your own words.

3 Re-read the dialogue about Mrs Bennet's nerves.

a Rewrite this dialogue in modern-day language.

b What does this conversation reveal about Mr and Mrs Bennet's relationship?

Extended reading

Compare how two writers use dialogue to convey a character's state of mind, focusing on the characters of Miss Brodie and Mrs Bennet. Think about:

■ what the characters say and how they say it

■ how this conveys the characters' thoughts and emotions

■ how to support your ideas with references to both texts.

Extended writing

Write a scene from a crime story where a detective investigates a murder suspect. As you write, think about:

■ the crime that has been committed and why the suspect is under suspicion

■ how the dialogue can move the plot of the story forward

■ the way dialogue can reveal the characters' thoughts and emotions

■ how you can use description to break up the dialogue, for example, describing the character's actions to emphasize or contradict what they say.

Remember to check the spelling, punctuation and grammar of your writing.

Early bird

How many different emotions can you suggest by rewriting this line?

'I'm fine,' she said.

You can change the dialogue tag or add descriptive details, but keep the dialogue the same. For example, 'I'm fine,' she sobbed, shaking her head.

Source texts table

Text	Date
9.1 'John Charrington's Wedding' by Edith Nesbit	1891
9.2 *Small Island* by Andrea Levy	2004
9.3 *The Princess Bride* by William Goldman	1973

Big picture

When you read a story, you are being guided on a path through the narrative by an invisible hand. The writer of the story is the person who decides the order in which scenes are shown to you as a reader. For example, the events of a story might be told in chronological order or the narrative might move about in time with flashbacks or flashforwards, depending on the effects the writer wants to create. Can you think of any stories you have read that are structured in interesting or unusual ways? In this section, you'll read extracts from novels written in the 19th, 20th and 21st centuries and explore how their writers use different structural features.

Skills

- Understand the meaning of a text

- Make inferences and refer to evidence in the text

- Explore how a writer's structural choices can create different effects

- Compare texts

- Use structural techniques to create specific effects in your own writing

Before reading

1a Think about a story you know well. This could be a book, a film or a video game.

Break the plot of the story down into its key events. For example, one student has begun to break down the plot of *The Hobbit* by J. R. R. Tolkien into the following events:

- Gandalf invites Bilbo to join him on a quest to regain the dwarves' treasure.

- Bilbo and the dwarves are captured by trolls but Gandalf frees them.

- When crossing the mountains, Bilbo and the dwarves take shelter in a cave but are captured by goblins.

1b Look back at your list of key events from the story. Can you identify a pivotal moment or climax that the story builds up to?

9.1 'John Charrington's Wedding' by Edith Nesbit, 1891

The following extract is taken from the short story 'John Charrington's Wedding'. The story recounts the events leading up to the wedding day of John Charrington and May Forster, a young couple living in a small English village in the late 19th century. The extract begins with the narrator, a man named Geoffrey, describing how he encountered John and May sitting together in the village churchyard. As you read the extract, note down how the narrative moves forward in time.

Source text 9.1

WORD BANK

Gladstone a small suitcase

I was coming home from the Club through the churchyard. Our church is on a thyme-grown hill, and the turf about it is so thick and soft that one's footsteps are noiseless.

I made no sound as I vaulted the low lichened wall, and threaded my way between the tombstones. It was at the same instant that I heard John Charrington's voice, and saw her face. May was sitting on a low flat gravestone with the full splendour of the western sun upon her *mignonne* face. Its expression ended, at once and for ever, any question of love for him; it was transfigured to a beauty I should not have believed possible, even to that beautiful little face.

John lay at her feet, and it was his voice that broke the stillness of the golden August evening.

'My dear, my dear, I believe I should come back from the dead if you wanted me!'

I coughed at once to indicate my presence, and passed on into the shadow fully enlightened.

The wedding was to be early in September. Two days before I had to run up to town on business. The train was late, of course, for we are on the South-Eastern, and as I stood grumbling with my watch in my hand, whom should I see but John Charrington and May Forster. They were walking up and down the unfrequented end of the platform, arm in arm, looking into each other's eyes, careless of the sympathetic interest of the porters.

Of course I knew better than to hesitate a moment before burying myself in the booking-office, and it was not till the train drew up at the platform, that I obtrusively passed the pair with my **Gladstone**, and took the corner in a first-class smoking-carriage. I did this with as good an air of not seeing them as I could assume. I pride myself on my discretion, but if John were travelling alone I wanted his company. I had it.

'Hullo, old man,' came his cheery voice as he swung his bag into my carriage; 'here's luck; I was expecting a dull journey!'

WORD BANK

Cain biblical character who was the brother of Abel

'Where are you off to?' I asked, discretion still bidding me turn my eyes away, though I saw, without looking, that hers were red-rimmed.

'To old Branbridge's,' he answered, shutting the door and leaning out for a last word with his sweetheart.

'Oh, I wish you wouldn't go, John,' she was saying in a low, earnest voice. 'I feel certain something will happen.'

'Do you think I should let anything happen to keep me, and the day after tomorrow our wedding-day?'

'Don't go,' she answered, with a pleading intensity which would have sent my Gladstone onto the platform and me after it. But she wasn't speaking to me. John Charrington was made differently: he rarely changed his opinions, never his resolutions.

He only stroked the little ungloved hands that lay on the carriage door.

'I must, May. The old boy's been awfully good to me, and now he's dying I must go and see him, but I shall come home in time for —' the rest of the parting was lost in a whisper and in the rattling lurch of the starting train.

'You're sure to come?' she spoke as the train moved.

'Nothing shall keep me,' he answered; and we steamed out. After he had seen the last of the little figure on the platform he leaned back in his corner and kept silence for a minute.

When he spoke it was to explain to me that his godfather, whose heir he was, lay dying at Peasmarsh Place, some fifty miles away, and had sent for John, and John had felt bound to go.

'I shall be surely back tomorrow,' he said, 'or, if not, the day after, in heaps of time. Thank Heaven, one hasn't to get up in the middle of the night to get married nowadays!'

'And suppose Mr Branbridge dies?'

'Alive or dead I mean to be married on Thursday!' John answered, lighting a cigar and unfolding *The Times*.

At Peasmarsh station we said 'goodbye', and he got out, and I saw him ride off; I went on to London, where I stayed the night.

When I got home the next afternoon, a very wet one, by the way, my sister greeted me with —

'Where's Charrington?'

'Goodness knows,' I answered testily. Every man, since **Cain**, has resented that kind of question.

'I thought you might have heard from him,' she went on, 'as you're to give him away tomorrow.'

'Isn't he back?' I asked, for I had confidently expected to find him at home.

'No, Geoffrey,' — my sister Fanny always had a way of jumping to conclusions, especially such conclusions as were least favourable to her fellow-creatures — 'he has not returned, and, what is more, you may depend upon it he won't. You mark my words, there'll be no wedding tomorrow.'

Basic reading skills

1   When the narrator encounters John and May in the churchyard, what does he see that convinces him that May truly loves John?

2   What does the narrator overhear John telling May in the churchyard?

3   Look again at the sentence, 'They were walking up and down the unfrequented end of the platform, arm in arm, looking into each other's eyes, careless of the sympathetic interest of the porters.' Explain what this suggests about John and May's feelings towards each other.

4   What reason does May give for not wishing John to go just before he leaves on the train?

5   Find a quotation that you think best indicates John's determination to be married.

1a This extract contains three scenes. Identify the time and location of each scene.

1b What connections can you find between the three scenes? Think about the characters' dialogue.

2a Pick a word that best describes the atmosphere created in the extract.

sinister

happy

foreboding

hopeful

dark

2b Select a quotation and explain how it helps to create this atmosphere.

3 How does the writer use language to suggest the strength of May's feelings for John? In your answer you should comment on:

- what May says and how she says it

- the way May is described.

4 What do you think the narrator's feelings towards May are? Find three quotations that suggest his feelings towards her and explain your choices.

9.2 *Small Island* by Andrea Levy, 2004

The following extract is taken from the novel *Small Island*. The novel is set in London in 1948. Here, Hortense, a Jamaican woman, has travelled to London to join her husband Gilbert, and has arrived at the house where she believes he is living. This prompts a memory from Hortense's childhood, so the extract begins with a flashback.

Source text 9.2

It brought it all back to me. Celia Langley. Celia Langley standing in front of me, her hands on her hips and her head in a cloud. And she is saying: 'Oh, Hortense, when I am older...' all her dreaming began with 'when I am older' '...when I am older, Hortense, I will be leaving Jamaica and I will be going to live in England.' This is when her voice became high-class and her nose point into the air – well, as far as her round flat nose could – and she swayed as she brought the picture to her mind's eye. 'Hortense, in England I will have a big house with a bell at the front door and I will ring the bell.' And she make the sound, ding-a-ling, ding-a-ling. 'I will ring the bell in this house when I am in England. That is what will happen to me when I am older.'

I said nothing at the time. I just nodded and said, 'You surely will, Celia Langley, you surely will.' I did not dare to dream that it would one day be I who would go to England. It would one day be I who would sail on a ship as big as a world and feel the sun's heat on my face gradually change from roasting to caressing. But there was I! Standing at the door of a house in London and ringing the bell. Pushing my finger to hear the ding-a-ling, ding-a-ling. Oh, Celia Langley, where were you then with your big ideas and your nose in the air? Could you see me? Could you see me there in London? Hortense Roberts married with a gold ring and a wedding dress in a trunk. Mrs Joseph. Mrs Gilbert Joseph. What you think of that, Celia Langley? There was I in England ringing the doorbell on one of the tallest houses I had ever seen.

But when I pressed this doorbell I did not hear a ring. No ding-a-ling, ding-a-ling. I pressed once more in case the doorbell was not operational. The house, I could see, was shabby. Mark you, shabby in a grand sort of a way. I was sure this house could once have been home to a doctor or a lawyer or perhaps a friend of a friend of the King. Only the house of someone high-class would have pillars at the doorway. Ornate pillars that twisted with elaborate design. The glass stained with coloured pictures as a church would have. It was true that some were missing, replaced by cardboard and strips of white tape. But who knows what devilish deeds Mr Hitler's bombs had carried out during the war? I pushed the doorbell again when it was obvious no one was answering my call. I held my thumb against it and pressed my ear to the window. A light came on now and a woman's voice started calling, 'All right, all right, I'm coming! Give us a minute.'

I stepped back down two steps avoiding a small lump of dog's business that rested in some litter and leaves. I straightened my coat, pulling it closed where I had unfortunately lost a button. I adjusted my hat in case it had sagged in the damp air and left me looking comical. I pulled my back up straight.

The door was answered by an Englishwoman. A blonde-haired, pink-cheeked Englishwoman with eyes so blue they were the brightest thing in the street. She looked on my face, parted her slender lips and said, 'Yes?'

'Is this the household of Mr Gilbert Joseph?'

'I beg your pardon?'

'Gilbert Joseph?' I said, a little slower.

'Oh, Gilbert. Who are you?' She pronounced Gilbert so strangely that for a moment I was anxious that I would be delivered to the wrong man.

'Mr Gilbert Joseph is my husband – I am his wife.'

The woman's face looked puzzled and pleased all at one time. She looked back into the house, lifting her head as she did. Then she turned back to me and said, 'Didn't he come to meet you?'

'I have not seen Gilbert,' I told her, then went on to ask, 'but this is **perchance** where he is **aboding**?'

At which this Englishwoman said, 'What?' She frowned and looked over my shoulder at the trunk, which was resting by the kerbside where it had been placed by the driver of the taxi vehicle. 'Is that yours?' she enquired.

'It is.'

'It's the size of the Isle of Wight. How did you get it here?' She laughed a little. A gentle giggle that played round her eyes and mouth.

I laughed too, so as not to give her the notion that I did not know what she was talking about as regards this 'white island'. I said, 'I came in a taxi cab and the driver assured me that this was the right address. Is this the house of Gilbert Joseph?'

The woman stood for a little while before answering by saying, 'Hang on here. I'll see if he's in his room.' She then shut the door in my face.

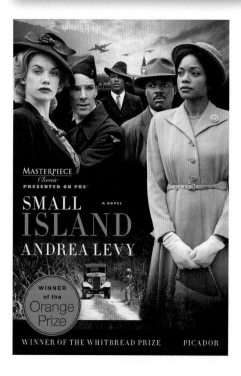

Basic reading skills

1   Where did Celia Langley say she was going to live when she was older?

2   Look again at the following sentence and explain what it suggests about Hortense's feelings towards Celia: 'Oh, Celia Langley, where were you then with your big ideas and your nose in the air?'

3   What three things does Hortense do when the woman calls out that she is coming to answer the door?

4   How does Hortense try to disguise the fact that she doesn't know what the woman is talking about when she says Hortense's trunk is 'the size of the Isle of Wight'?

Advanced reading skills

1   The extract begins with a flashback where Hortense looks back at an event from her childhood.

   a   What event does Hortense remember?

   b   Why does Hortense remember this now?

   c   Explain what the flashback helps you to understand about Hortense's character.

2   How do Hortense's emotions change during the extract? Pick out quotations that suggest her different emotions. For example, 'What do you think of that, Celia Langley?' – Proud.

3   Look at the following echo between the flashback and the present-day scene. Why do you think the writer makes this link? What does this suggest about the house Hortense is calling at?

   Flashback: 'And she make the sound, ding-a-ling, ding-a-ling.'

   Present day: 'No ding-a-ling, ding-a-ling.'

4   Re-read the conversation between Hortense and the woman who answers the door. How is the conversation structured to give you an impression of these two characters? You should comment on:

   ■   how the woman is described from Hortense's point of view

   ■   how Hortense speaks to the woman

   ■   how the woman speaks and acts towards Hortense

   ■   the way the extract ends.

9.3 *The Princess Bride* by William Goldman, 1973

The following text is an extract from the novel *The Princess Bride*. This novel is a fantasy story about a young woman named Buttercup who has agreed to marry the Crown Prince, as she believes her true love Westley has been killed by the Dread Pirate Roberts. In the novel, the story of *The Princess Bride* is being read by a father to his son, which gives it an unusual structure. In the following extract, Buttercup has been kidnapped by a trio of bandits at night and has jumped into the sea in an attempt to escape, while the kidnappers search for her in the dark.

Source text 9.3

'Princess,' the Sicilian called, 'do you know what happens to sharks when they smell blood in the water? They go mad. There is no controlling their wildness. They rip and shred and chew and devour, and I'm in a boat, Princess, and there isn't any blood in the water now, so we're both quite safe, but there is a knife in my hand, my lady, and if you don't come back I'll cut my arms and I'll cut my legs and I'll catch the blood in a cup and I'll fling it as far as I can and sharks can smell blood in the water for miles and you won't be beautiful for long.'

Buttercup hesitated, silently treading water. Around her now, although it was surely her imagination, she seemed to be hearing the swish of giant tails.

'Come back and come back now. There will be no other warning.'

Buttercup thought, If I come back, they'll kill me anyway, so what's the difference?

'The difference is—'

There he goes doing that again, thought Buttercup. He really *is* a mind reader.

'—if you come back now,' the Sicilian went on, 'I give you my word as a gentleman and assassin that you will die totally without pain. I assure you, you will get no such promise from the sharks.'

The fish sounds in the night were closer now.

Buttercup began to tremble with fear. She was terribly ashamed of herself but there it was. She only wished she could see for a minute if there really were sharks and if he would really cut himself.

The Sicilian winced out loud.

'He's just cut his arm, lady,' the Turk called out. 'He's catching the blood in a cup now. There must be a half-inch of blood on the bottom.'

The Sicilian winced again.

'He cut his leg this time,' the Turk went on. 'The cup's getting full.'

I don't believe them, Buttercup thought. There are no sharks in the water and there is no blood in his cup.

'My arm is back to throw,' the Sicilian said. 'Call out your location or not, the choice is yours.'

I'm not making a peep, Buttercup decided.

'Farewell,' from the Sicilian.

There was the splashing sound of liquid landing on liquid.

Then there came a pause.

Then the sharks went mad—

* * *

'She does not get eaten by the sharks at this time,' my father said.

I looked up at him. 'What?'

'You looked like you were getting too involved and bothered so I thought I would let you relax.'

'Oh, for Pete's sake,' I said, 'you'd think I was a baby or something. What kind of stuff is that?' I really sounded put out, but I'll tell you the truth: I was getting a little too involved and I was glad he told me. I mean, when you're a kid, you don't think, Well, since the book's called The Princess Bride *and since we're barely into it, obviously, the author's not about to make shark kibble of his leading lady. You get hooked on things when you're a youngster, so to any youngsters reading, I'll simply repeat my father's words since they worked to soothe me: 'She does not get eaten by the sharks at this time.'*

* * *

Then the sharks went mad. All around her, Buttercup could hear them beeping and screaming and thrashing their mighty tails. Nothing can save me, Buttercup realized. I'm a dead cookie.

Fortunately for all concerned save the sharks, it was around this time that the moon came out.

'There she is,' shouted the Sicilian, and like lightning the Spaniard turned the boat and as the boat drew close the Turk reached out a giant arm and then she was back in the safety of her murderers while all around them the sharks bumped each other in wild frustration.

Basic reading skills

1   Re-read the opening paragraph. What does the Sicilian say he will do if Buttercup, who he calls Princess, does not come back?

2   'Buttercup thought, If I come back, they'll kill me anyway, so what's the difference?' What promise does the Sicilian make to persuade Buttercup that there is a difference?

3a Choose one word from the list below that you think best describes how Buttercup is feeling.

calm   fearful   confused   cautious   optimistic

3b Select a quotation that you think suggests this emotion. Give reasons for your choice.

4 '"She does not get eaten by sharks at this time," my father said.' Why does the father interrupt the story to tell his son this?

5 Re-read the final paragraph of the extract. Explain what the phrase 'back in the safety of her murderers' suggests about Buttercup's situation.

Advanced reading skills

1 How does the writer build tension in the opening section, which describes the bandits in the boat and Buttercup in the water? Comment on:

- the writer's use of dialogue and the effect this creates

- the writer's use of language to present Buttercup's thoughts and emotions

- the sequence of events in this section and the way the action is presented.

2 Look at the following student's comment about the structure of this extract.

I find it annoying that the writer interrupts the story just when it's getting really scary.

a Do you agree or disagree with this student's comment? Refer to the text to support your point of view.

b Why do you think the writer introduces the conversation between the narrator and his father at this point? Think about:

- what impression this gives you about the narrator and his father

- what you learn about their relationship from this section.

3 Narrative pace is the speed at which a story is told. Re-read the section from 'Then the sharks went mad. All around her ...' to the end of the extract. How would you describe the narrative pace of this section of the extract? You should comment on:

- the length of the sentences and paragraphs, and the impact these have on the narrative pace

- the balance between action, description and dialogue in this section and the effect this creates.

4 Read the following quotation from the introduction to *The Princess Bride*: 'My father only read me the action stuff, the good parts.'

Explain whether you think this extract supports or contradicts this statement. Give reasons for your answer, referring to the text of the extract.

Extended reading

Compare the extracts you have read from *Small Island* and *The Princess Bride* in order to answer the following question.

Compare how the two writers use structure to build tension. In your answer, you should:

■ identify the sources of tension in both extracts

■ compare the structural choices each writer makes

■ explore how these help to build tension

■ support your ideas with references to both texts.

Extended writing

Look again at the extract from *The Princess Bride*. Write a new conversation between the narrator and his father that follows on from the end of the extract. As you write, think about:

■ the reason the father or narrator could give for interrupting the story again at this point

■ how the other character would respond

■ what their dialogue could reveal about their thoughts and feelings about Buttercup's rescue

■ what their dialogue could suggest about their relationship.

Remember to check the spelling, punctuation and grammar of your writing.

Early bird

In Marcel Proust's novel *In Search of Lost Time*, the taste of madeleine cake triggers the narrator to recall a childhood memory. Think of other objects and things that could trigger a flashback and suggest what this memory might be about. Some examples have been started below.

■ A box of matches – *A retired firefighter remembering a terrifying fire she once fought.*

■ A sandcastle being washed away by the incoming tide –

Source texts table

Text	Date
10.1 *The Dark is Rising* by Susan Cooper	1973
10.2 *The Picture of Dorian Gray* by Oscar Wilde	1890
10.3 *City of the Beasts* by Isabel Allende	2002

Big picture

Fiction is about ideas. From love and money to power and lies, the **themes** that run through a story can help readers to explore big ideas about life and understand more about themselves. Looking beneath the surface of a story can help you to identify its deeper themes. Think about your favourite stories; what themes do they contain? In this section you'll read extracts from novels from the 19th, 20th and 21st centuries, and explore their themes.

Skills

- Understand the meaning of a text
- Make inferences and refer to evidence in the text
- Explore the use of imagery, **symbols** and **motifs** to convey theme
- Study how setting, plot and characterization are established
- Use techniques explored in reading to convey a theme in your own writing

Before reading

1   Think about the last book you read. What themes do you think it contained? Look at the list below for some ideas.

friendship   family   power   love   revenge   technology

growing up   heroism   identity   injustice   nature

Key terms

theme an idea that emerges from a literary work's treatment of its subject-matter or a topic that recurs in it

symbol something representing or standing for something else (often a physical thing representing something non-physical)

motif an image that is repeated in a literary work

connotation an idea or meaning suggested by a word or phrase

2   Identify the themes of the following Shakespeare plays:
- *Romeo and Juliet*
- *The Tempest*
- *Twelfth Night*
- *A Midsummer Night's Dream*
- *Julius Caesar*
- *Macbeth*
- *Much Ado About Nothing*

3   A motif is an image that is repeated in a story and can indicate the story's theme. For example, if imagery relating to darkness is repeated in a text, this motif could suggest that the theme is about death as this is a common **connotation**. What themes do you think the following motifs could suggest? Give reasons for your answers.

heart   mirror   bridge   blood   eyes

10.1 *The Dark is Rising* by Susan Cooper, 1973

The following extract is taken from the novel *The Dark is Rising* by Susan Cooper. This fantasy novel is about a boy called Will who is drawn into an ancient battle between forces of good and evil. Here, Will is walking home through the countryside with his brother James on the way back from their neighbour's farm, when he spots a stranger whom he also noticed on their way there. As you read, think about how the images in the extract could suggest the theme of good versus evil.

Source text 10.1

WORD BANK

rookery a nesting place for birds such as crows or rooks

The noise from the **rookery** was louder, even though the daylight was beginning to die. They could see the dark birds thronging over the treetops, more agitated than before, flapping and turning to and fro. And Will had been right; there was a stranger in the lane, standing beside the churchyard.

He was a shambling, tattered figure, more like a bundle of old clothes than a man, and at the sight of him the boys slowed their pace and drew instinctively closer to the cart and to one another. He turned his shaggy head to look at them.

Then suddenly, in a dreadful blur of unreality, a hoarse, shrieking flurry was rushing dark down out of the sky, and two huge rooks swooped at the man. He staggered back, shouting, his hands thrust up to protect his face, and the birds flapped their great wings in a black vicious whirl and were gone, swooping up past the boys and into the sky.

Will and James stood frozen, staring, pressed against the bales of hay.

The stranger cowered back against the gate.

'Kaaaaaak... kaaaaaak...' came the head-splitting racket from the frenzied flock over the wood, and then three more whirling black shapes were swooping after the first two, diving wildly at the man and then away. This time he screamed in terror and stumbled out into the road, his arms still wrapped in defence round his head, his face down; and he ran. The boys heard the frightened gasps for breath as he dashed headlong past them, and up the road past the gates of Dawsons' Farm and on towards the village. They saw bushy, greasy grey hair below a dirty old cap; a torn brown overcoat tied with string, and some other garment flapping beneath it; old boots, one with a loose sole that made him kick his leg oddly sideways, half-hopping, as he ran. But they did not see his face.

The high whirling above their heads was dwindling into loops of slow flight, and the rooks began to settle one by one into the trees. They were still talking to one another in a long cawing jumble, but the madness and the violence were not in it now. Dazed, moving his head for the first time, Will felt his cheek brush against something, and putting his hand to his shoulder, he found a long black feather there. He pushed it into his jacket pocket, moving slowly, like someone half-awake.

Together they pushed the loaded cart down the road to the house, and the cawing behind them died to an ominous murmur, like the swollen Thames in spring.

Basic reading skills

1   Re-read the opening paragraph.

   a List one thing that Will and James hear.

   b List two things that Will and James see.

2   List three details about the stranger.

3   When the rooks first attack the man this is described as happening in 'a dreadful blur of unreality'. Explain in your own words what this phrase means.

4   What does Will put into his pocket?

5   Summarize in a sentence how Will reacts to the attack.

Advanced reading skills

1   How do you think Will and James feel about the stranger when they first see him? Refer to evidence from the text to support your answer.

2   *The Dark is Rising* deals with the theme of good and evil. From the extract, choose a motif that you think symbolizes good and a motif that you think symbolizes evil. Explain your choices.

3   Re-read the paragraph beginning 'Then suddenly, in a dreadful blur of unreality...' How does the writer's use of language emphasize the ferocity of the rooks' attack? In your answer you should comment on the writer's choice of verbs, adjectives and imagery and the effects that these create.

4   Re-read the paragraph beginning 'Kaaaaaaak... kaaaaaak...' How does the writer's use of language emphasize the man's fear? In your answer you should comment on the man's actions and the way these are described.

5   Based on what you have read, explain why you think the rooks attacked the stranger. Support your answer with reference to the text.

10.2 *The Picture of Dorian Gray* by Oscar Wilde, 1890

The following extract is taken from the novel *The Picture of Dorian Gray*. In this novel, a handsome man named Dorian Gray has his portrait painted and, fearing that his beauty will fade over time, sells his soul to ensure that while he stays forever youthful his portrait will age and fade instead. Here, Dorian reveals the hideous portrait to his friend Basil Hallward, the artist who painted it originally. As you read, think about what the themes of the story could be.

Source text 10.2

He passed out of the room and began the ascent, Basil Hallward following close behind. They walked softly, as men do instinctively at night. The lamp cast fantastic shadows on the wall and staircase. A rising wind made some of the windows rattle.

When they reached the top landing, Dorian set the lamp down on the floor, and taking out the key turned it in the lock. 'You insist on knowing, Basil?' he asked, in a low voice.

'Yes.'

'I am delighted,' he answered, smiling. Then he added, somewhat harshly, 'You are the one man in the world who is entitled to know everything about me. You have had more to do with my life than you think'; and, taking up the lamp, he opened the door and went in. A cold current of air passed them, and the light shot up for a moment in a flame of murky orange. He shuddered. 'Shut the door behind you,' he whispered, as he placed the lamp on the table.

cassone an ornamental chest

wainscoting wooden panelling that lines the lower part of the walls of a room

vermilion bright red

parody an exaggerated imitation of the style of a particular artist, writer, composer or performer

ignoble dishonourable

satire humour or exaggeration used to show what is bad or weak about a person or thing

Hallward glanced round him, with a puzzled expression. The room looked as if it had not been lived in for years. A faded Flemish tapestry, a curtained picture, an old Italian **cassone**, and an almost empty bookcase—that was all that it seemed to contain, besides a chair and a table. As Dorian Gray was lighting a half-burned candle that was standing on the mantelshelf, he saw that the whole place was covered with dust, and that the carpet was in holes. A mouse ran scuffling behind the **wainscoting**. There was a damp odour of mildew.

'So you think that it is only God who sees the soul, Basil? Draw that curtain back, and you will see mine.'

The voice that spoke was cold and cruel. 'You are mad, Dorian, or playing a part,' muttered Hallward, frowning.

'You won't? Then I must do it myself,' said the young man; and he tore the curtain from its rod, and flung it on the ground.

An exclamation of horror broke from the painter's lips as he saw in the dim light the hideous face on the canvas grinning at him. There was something in its expression that filled him with disgust and loathing. Good heavens! it was Dorian Gray's own face that he was looking at! The horror, whatever it was, had not yet entirely spoiled that marvellous beauty. There was still some gold in the thinning hair and some scarlet on the sensual mouth. The sodden eyes had kept something of the loveliness of their blue, the noble curves had not yet completely passed away from chiselled nostrils and from plastic throat. Yes, it was Dorian himself. But who had done it? He seemed to recognize his own brushwork, and the frame was his own design. The idea was monstrous, yet he felt afraid. He seized the lighted candle, and held it to the picture. In the left-hand corner was his own name, traced in long letters of bright **vermilion**.

It was some foul **parody**, some infamous **ignoble satire**. He had never done that. Still, it was his own picture. He knew it, and he felt as if his blood had changed in a moment from fire to sluggish ice. His own picture! What did it mean? Why had it altered? He turned, and looked at Dorian Gray with the eyes of a sick man. His mouth twitched, and his parched tongue seemed unable to articulate. He passed his hand across his forehead. It was dank with clammy sweat.

The young man was leaning against the mantelshelf, watching him with that strange expression that one sees on the faces of those who are absorbed in a play when some great artist is acting. There was neither real sorrow in it nor real joy. There was simply the passion of the spectator, with perhaps a flicker of triumph in his eyes. He had taken the flower out of his coat, and was smelling it, or pretending to do so.

'What does this mean?' cried Hallward, at last. His own voice sounded shrill and curious in his ears.

'Years ago, when I was a boy,' said Dorian Gray, crushing the flower in his hand, 'you met me, flattered me, and taught me to be vain of my good looks. One day you introduced me to a friend of yours, who explained to me the wonder of youth, and you finished a portrait of me that revealed to me the wonder of beauty. In a mad moment, that, even now, I don't know whether I regret or not, I made a wish, perhaps you would call it a prayer...'

'I remember it! Oh, how well I remember it! No! the thing is impossible. The room is damp. Mildew has got into the canvas. The paints I used had some wretched mineral poison in them. I tell you the thing is impossible.'

'Ah, what is impossible?' murmured the young man, going over to the window, and leaning his forehead against the cold, mist-stained glass.

'You told me you had destroyed it.'

'I was wrong. It has destroyed me.'

1   Where does Dorian keep his portrait?

2   'The room looked as if it had not been lived in for years.' List three details about the room that suggest this.

3a How does Basil react when he sees Dorian's portrait?

3b Explain why Basil has this reaction to Dorian's portrait.

4   List the two explanations Basil suggests for why Dorian's portrait looks like it does.

5   Re-read the final lines. Explain what you think Dorian means when he says about his portrait, 'It has destroyed me.'

1   What impression do you get of Dorian Gray from this extract? Think about:

   ■ Dorian's dialogue and the way he speaks

   ■ Dorian's actions and reactions, and the way these are described

   ■ how his portrait is described and what this suggests about his character

   ■ how Basil reacts to both Dorian and his portrait.

Key term

foreshadowing a literary technique where words and phrases are used to hint about what is going to happen in the story

2   Look again at the paragraph beginning 'Hallward glanced round him, with a puzzled expression' and explain how this **foreshadows** the unveiling of Dorian's portrait.

3   Re-read the paragraph beginning 'An exclamation of horror broke from the painter's lips...'. Comment on how the writer's use of sentence forms conveys Basil's reaction to the portrait. You should comment on the effects created by:

   ■ the use of multi-clause sentences

   ■ the use of exclamations and a question.

4a Re-read the extract and note any words or imagery linked with decay or disrepair.

4b One of the themes of *The Picture of Dorian Gray* is youth versus age. Explain how the writer's use of the motif of decay reflects this theme.

10.3 *City of the Beasts* by Isabel Allende, 2002

The following extract is taken from the novel *City of the Beasts* by Isabel Allende. Here, Alexander Cold, a 15-year-old boy whose mother has been diagnosed with cancer, wakes up in his family home in a small Californian town in the United States of America. As you read, think about what the themes of the story could be.

Source text 10.3

Alexander Cold awakened at dawn, startled by a nightmare. He had been dreaming that an enormous black bird had crashed against the window with a clatter of shattered glass, flown into the house, and carried off his mother. In the dream, he watched helplessly as the gigantic vulture clasped Lisa Cold's clothing in its yellow claws, flew out the same broken window, and disappeared into a sky heavy with dark clouds. What had awakened him was the noise from the storm: wind lashing the trees, rain on the rooftop, and thunder.

He turned on the light with the sensation of being adrift in a boat, and pushed closer to the bulk of the large dog sleeping beside him. He pictured the roaring Pacific Ocean a few blocks from his house, spilling in furious waves against the cliffs. He lay listening to the storm and thinking about the black bird and about his mother, waiting for the pounding in his chest to die down. He was still tangled in the images of his bad dream.

Alexander looked at the clock: six-thirty, time to get up. Outside, it was beginning to get light. He decided that this was going to be a terrible day, one of those days when it's best to stay in bed because everything is going to turn out bad. There had been a lot of days like that since his mother got sick; sometimes the air in the house felt heavy, like being at the bottom of the sea. On those days, the only relief was to escape, to run along the beach with Poncho until he was out of breath. But it had been raining and raining for more than a week—a real deluge—and on top of that, Poncho had been bitten by a deer and didn't want to move. Alex was convinced that he had the dumbest dog in history, the only eighty-pound Labrador ever bitten by a deer. In the four years of his life, Poncho had been attacked by raccoons, the neighbor's cat, and now a deer—not counting the times he had been sprayed by the skunks and they'd had to bathe him in tomato juice to get rid of the smell. Alex got out of bed without disturbing Poncho and got dressed, shivering; the heat came on at six, but it hadn't yet warmed his room, the one at the end of the hall.

At breakfast Alex was not in the mood to applaud his father's efforts at making pancakes. John Cold was not exactly a good cook; the only thing he knew how to do was pancakes, and they always turned out like rubber-tire tortillas. His children didn't want to hurt his feelings, so they pretended to eat them, but anytime he wasn't looking, they spit them out into the garbage pail. They had tried in vain to train Poncho to eat them: the dog was stupid, but not that stupid.

'When's Momma going to get better?' Nicole asked, trying to spear a rubbery pancake with her fork.

'Shut up, Nicole!' Alex replied, tired of hearing his younger sister ask the same question several times a week.

'Momma's going to die,' Andrea added.

'Liar! She's not going to die!' shrieked Nicole.

'You two are just kids. You don't know what you're talking about!' Alex exclaimed.

'Here, girls. Quiet now. Momma is going to get better,' John interrupted, without much conviction.

Alex was angry with his father, his sisters, Poncho, life in general—even with his mother for getting sick. He rushed out of the kitchen, ready to leave without breakfast, but he tripped over the dog in the hallway and sprawled flat.

'Get out of my way, you stupid dog!' he yelled, and Poncho, delighted, gave him a loud slobbery kiss that left Alex's glasses spattered with saliva.

Basic reading skills

1   Re-read the opening paragraph.

   a Using your own words, summarize Alexander's dream.

   b What has woken Alexander up?

2   'He was still tangled in the images of his bad dream.' Explain what this sentence means.

3   List three reasons why Alexander might think 'he had the dumbest dog in history'.

4a   Which of Alexander's sisters says that their mother is going to die?

4b   Are Alexander's sisters younger or older than him? Find evidence from the text to support your answer.

5   Why does Alexander rush out of the kitchen?

Advanced reading skills

1   A symbol represents or stands for something else. Re-read the opening paragraph and explain what you think the vulture in Alexander's dream symbolizes.

2   What impression do you get of Alexander from this extract?

3   Which of the following themes do you think lie beneath the surface of this extract? Justify your choices with reference to the text.

family   love   growing up   nature
friendship   death

Extended reading

Choose two of the extracts you have read in this section and make notes about how each text uses imagery, symbols and motifs to convey its theme or themes.

Now compare your two chosen extracts. In your comparison you should:

■   identify any similarities and differences between the themes explored and the techniques used to convey these

■   explore how you respond to the themes presented as a reader

■   evaluate which extract you think is the most successful in conveying its themes and why.

Extended writing

Write the opening of a story that explores one of the following themes:

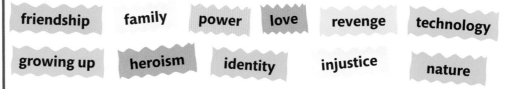

friendship   family   power   love   revenge   technology
growing up   heroism   identity   injustice   nature

As you write, think about how you can draw on different techniques from the three texts you have read to convey your chosen theme.

Remember to check the spelling, punctuation and grammar of your writing.

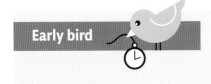

Early bird

Decide what themes the following symbols could represent:

a broken mirror   a ladder   blood   a ring   a storm

Invent your own symbols for the following themes:

power   revenge   identity   injustice   nature

Source texts table

Text	Date
11.1 *Pigeon English* by Stephen Kelman	2011
11.2 *The Woman in Black* by Susan Hill	1983
11.3 *Great Expectations* by Charles Dickens	1861

Big picture

When you read fiction, the words a writer chooses to describe characters, settings and the events of a story create pictures in your mind. Have you ever watched a film version of one of your favourite books? Did the scenes shown on screen match the ones you imagined when you read the book? In this section you will read extracts from novels written in the 19th, 20th and 21st centuries and explore the techniques their authors use to create effective descriptions.

Skills

- Make inferences and refer to evidence in the text

- Explore how writers use language and structure to create effective descriptions

- Compare writers' descriptive techniques and the effects these create

- Use techniques explored in reading to create effective descriptions in your own writing

Before reading

1   Look at the following extract from a letter written by the author C. S. Lewis about how to write an effective description:

Source text

Don't use adjectives which merely tell us how you want us to feel about the thing you are describing. I mean, instead of telling us a thing was 'terrible,' describe it so that we'll be terrified. Don't say it was 'delightful'; make us say 'delightful' when we've read the description. You see, all those words (horrifying, wonderful, hideous, exquisite) are only like saying to your readers, 'Please will you do my job for me.'

Do you think this is helpful advice? Discuss your ideas about the advice.

2   Look back at a recent short story or description you have written.

   a   Highlight any adjectives which you think tell the reader how you want them to feel about the thing you are describing.

   b   Using a different colour, highlight any descriptive details that you think follow C. S. Lewis's advice.

11.1 *Pigeon English* by Stephen Kelman, 2011

The following text is taken from the novel *Pigeon English* by Stephen Kelman. Set in present-day London, the novel is about Harrison Opuku, an 11-year-old boy who has recently arrived in Britain from Ghana and whose life is changed forever when one of his friends is murdered. Here, Harrison and his friend Jordan visit the spot where the boy was killed. As you read the description of the murder scene, think about how Harrison seems to feel about his friend's death.

You could see the blood. It was darker than you thought. It was all on the ground outside Chicken Joe's. It just felt crazy.

Jordan: 'I'll give you a million quid if you touch it.'

Me: 'You don't have a million.'

Jordan: 'One quid then.'

You wanted to touch it but you couldn't get close enough. There was a line in the way:

POLICE LINE DO NOT CROSS

If you cross the line you'll turn to dust.

We weren't allowed to talk to the policeman, he had to concentrate for if the killer came back. I could see the chains hanging from his belt but I couldn't see the gun.

The dead boy's mamma was guarding the blood. She wanted it to stay, you could tell. The rain wanted to come and wash the blood away but she wouldn't let it. She wasn't even crying, she was just stiff and fierce like it was her job to scare the rain back up into the sky. A pigeon was looking for his chop. He walked right in the blood. He was even sad as well, you could tell where his eyes were all pink and dead.

The flowers were already bent. There were pictures of the dead boy wearing his school uniform. His jumper was green.

My jumper's blue. My uniform's better. The only bad thing about it is the tie, it's too scratchy. I hate it when they're scratchy like that.

There were bottles of beer instead of candles and the dead boy's friends wrote messages to him. They all said he was a great friend. Some of the spelling was wrong but I didn't mind. His football boots were on the railings tied up by their laces. They were nearly new Nikes, the studs were proper metal and everything.

Jordan: 'Shall I t'ief them? He don't need 'em no more.'

I just pretended I didn't hear him. Jordan would never really steal them, they were a million times too big. They looked too empty just hanging there. I wanted to wear them but they'd never fit.

Me and the dead boy were only half friends, I didn't see him very much because he was older and he didn't go to my school. He could ride his bike with no hands and you never even wanted him to fall off. I said a prayer for him inside my head. It just said sorry. That's all I could remember. I pretended like if I kept looking hard enough I could make the blood move and go back in the shape of a boy. I could bring him back alive that way. It happened before, where I used to live there was a chief who brought his son back like that. It was a long time ago, before I was born. **Asweh**, it was a miracle. It didn't work this time.

I gave him my bouncy ball. I don't need it anymore, I've got five more under my bed. Jordan only gave him a pebble he found on the floor.

Me: 'That doesn't count. It has to be something that belonged to you.'

Jordan: 'I ain't got nothing. I didn't know we had to bring a present.'

I gave Jordan a strawberry Chewit to give to the dead boy, then I showed him how to make a cross. Both the two of us made a cross. We were very quiet. It even felt important. We ran all the way home. I beat Jordan easily. I can beat everybody, I'm the fastest in Year 7. I just wanted to get away before the dying caught us.

WORD BANK

Asweh Ghanaian slang meaning 'I swear'

'This boy's love letter to the world made me laugh and tremble all the way through' Emma Donoghue

'A powerful and impressive novel ... Utterly convincing and deeply moving' Clare Morrall

PIGEON ENGLISH

STEPHEN KELMAN

BLOOMSBURY

Basic reading skills

1. What does Jordan say he will give Harrison if he touches the blood?

2. 'It just felt crazy.' What do you think Harrison means by this?

3. Pick out three details about the dead boy's mother. What do these details suggest about her feelings?

4. Re-read the paragraph beginning 'Me and the dead boy were only half friends…' What emotions is Harrison feeling here? Support your answer with reference to the text.

5. Draw a simple sketch of the scene described in this extract. Use quotations from the text to label any specific details in your sketch.

6. Re-read the final paragraph. Explain why Harrison runs all the way home.

Advanced reading skills

Key term

hyperbole a deliberately exaggerated statement that is not meant to be taken literally

1. Re-read the opening paragraph. What does the writer focus on here and how does this make you feel? You should comment on:
   - the words and phrases chosen and the effects these create
   - the sentence forms and patterns used in this opening paragraph
   - how the description makes you feel as a reader.

2. Find an example of **hyperbole** from the extract and explain the effect this creates.

3a. Which of the following words would you use to describe the atmosphere created in this extract?

grim   sad   gritty   fearful   tense   mournful   mysterious

3b. Pick out three examples of vocabulary that you think help to create this atmosphere. Explain your choices, exploring the connotations of the words you have selected.

3c. Pick out one sentence form that you think helps to create this atmosphere. Explain your choice, exploring the way the sentence is structured and the punctuation used.

4. What effect does the writer's use of second-person pronouns create in the following sentences?

> 'You could see the blood. It was darker than you thought.'
>
> 'You wanted to touch it but you couldn't get close enough.'
>
> 'If you cross the line you'll turn to dust.'

11.2 *The Woman in Black* by Susan Hill, 1983

The following extract is taken from the novel *The Woman in Black* by Susan Hill. This novel is about Arthur Kipps, a junior solicitor, who has to stay at the desolate and secluded Eel Marsh House to sort through the papers of its owner, Mrs Drablow, who has recently died. Here, the narrator Arthur Kipps is awakened by the sound of a child's cry, even though the house is empty. As you read the description, think about the emotions the author wants you to feel.

Source text 11.2

WORD BANK

bearings to work out where you are, the direction or position of one thing in relation to another

conjecture guesswork or a guess

the woman in black a mysterious figure seen by the narrator

retainer a servant who has worked for a person or family for a long time

rational reasonable or sane

Samuel Daily a local landowner who has left his dog, Spider, with Arthur Kipps

As I went out onto the landing, Spider the dog following me at once, two things happened together. I had the impression of someone who had just that very second before gone past me on their way from the top of the stairs to one of the other rooms, and, as a tremendous blast of wind hit the house so that it all but seemed to rock at the impact, the lights went out. I had not bothered to pick up my torch from the bedside table and now I stood in the pitch blackness, unsure for a moment of my **bearings**.

And the person who had gone by, and who was now in this house with me? I had seen no one, felt nothing. There had been no movement, no brush of a sleeve against mine, no disturbance of the air, I had not even heard a footstep. I had simply the absolutely certain sense of someone just having passed close to me and gone away down the corridor. Down the short narrow corridor that led to the nursery whose door had been so firmly locked and then, inexplicably, opened.

For a moment I actually began to **conjecture** that there was indeed someone – another human being – living here in this house, a person who hid themselves away in that mysterious nursery and came out at night to fetch food and drink and to take the air. Perhaps it was **the woman in black**? Had Mrs Drablow harboured some reclusive old sister or **retainer**, had she left behind her a mad friend that no one had known about? My brain span all manner of wild, incoherent fantasies as I tried desperately to provide a **rational** explanation for the presence I had been so aware of. But then they ceased. There was no living occupant of Eel Marsh House other than myself and **Samuel Daily**'s dog. Whatever was about, whoever I had seen, and heard rocking, and who had passed me by just now, whoever had opened the locked door was not 'real'. No. But what *was* 'real'? At that moment I began to doubt my own reality.

The first thing I must have was a light and I groped my way back across to my bed, reached over it and got my hand to the torch at last, took a step back, stumbled over the dog who was at my heels and dropped the torch. It went spinning away across the floor and fell somewhere by the window with a crash and the faint sound of breaking glass. I cursed but managed, by crawling about on my hands and knees, to find it again and to press the switch. No light came on. The torch had broken.

For a moment I was as near to weeping tears of despair and fear, frustration and tension, as I had ever been since my childhood. But instead of crying I drummed my fists upon the floorboards, in a burst of violent rage, until they throbbed.

It was Spider who brought me to my senses by scratching a little at my arm and then by licking the hand I stretched out to her. We sat on the floor together and I hugged her warm body to me, glad of her, thoroughly ashamed of myself, calmer and relieved, while the wind boomed and roared without, and again and again I heard that child's terrible cry borne on the gusts towards me.

Basic reading skills

1 Re-read the first paragraph.

   a The narrator has the impression of someone going past him on the landing. List two other things that happen when he goes out onto the landing.

   b What does the narrator forget to take with him onto the landing?

2 Now re-read the second paragraph.

   a List the four pieces of evidence the narrator gives that might cause him to doubt whether there is anyone else in the house.

   b Select a quotation that shows that the narrator is convinced that he is not alone.

3 'My brain span all manner of wild, incoherent fantasies as I tried desperately to provide a rational explanation for the presence I had been so aware of.' Using your own words, explain what this sentence means.

4 Write a summary of the events described in the extract.

Advanced reading skills

1. Look again at the opening paragraph. How does the way the writer has structured this paragraph help to give you the impression of everything happening at once? Think about:

   - the order in which information is given

   - the writer's choice of sentence forms

   - the writer's use of conjunctions.

2. Look again at the paragraph beginning 'The first thing I must have was a light...' Identify the verbs the narrator uses to describe the action of this paragraph and explain the impression they create of his state of mind.

3. Read what this student says about the text:

   I think this description shows that fear is all in the mind.

   Explain what you think this student means. Do you agree or disagree with this point of view? Find evidence from the text to support your viewpoint.

4. Compare the extracts from *Pigeon English* and *The Woman in Black*. Copy and complete a table like the one below to collect your ideas.

Feature	*Pigeon English*	*The Woman in Black*
Narrative viewpoint		
Vocabulary		
Mood (i.e. the tone or atmosphere conveyed)		
Sentence forms and structures		

11.3 *Great Expectations* by Charles Dickens, 1861

The following extract is taken from the novel *Great Expectations* by Charles Dickens, which was first published in 1861. Here, Pip, a young orphan boy who lives with his sister and brother-in-law, has been taken to visit Miss Havisham, a rich spinster who lives nearby. As you read, think about the impression you get of Miss Havisham from Dickens's description of her.

Source text 11.3

I entered, therefore, and found myself in a pretty large room, well lighted with wax candles. No glimpse of daylight was to be seen in it. It was a dressing-room, as I supposed from the furniture, though much of it was of forms and uses then quite unknown to me. But **prominent** in it was a draped table with a gilded **looking-glass**, and that I made out at first sight to be a fine lady's dressing-table.

Whether I should have made out this object so soon if there had been no fine lady sitting at it, I cannot say. In an armchair, with an elbow resting on the table and her head leaning on that hand, sat the strangest lady I have ever seen, or shall ever see.

She was dressed in rich materials—satins, and lace, and silks—all of white. Her shoes were white. And she had a long white veil dependent from her hair, and she had bridal flowers in her hair, but her hair was white. Some bright jewels sparkled on her neck and on her hands, and some other jewels lay sparkling on the table. Dresses, less splendid than the dress she wore, and half-packed trunks, were scattered about. She had not quite finished dressing, for she had but one shoe on—the other was on the table near her hand—her veil was but half arranged, her watch and chain were not put on, and some lace for her bosom lay with those trinkets, and with her handkerchief, and gloves, and some flowers, and a prayer-book all confusedly heaped about the looking-glass.

It was not in the first few moments that I saw all these things, though I saw more of them in the first moments than might be supposed. But I saw that everything within my view which ought to be white, had been white long ago, and had lost its **lustre** and was faded and yellow. I saw that the bride within the bridal dress had withered like the dress, and like the flowers, and had no brightness left but the brightness of her sunken eyes. I saw that the dress had been put upon the rounded figure of a young woman, and that the figure upon which it now hung loose had shrunk to skin and bone. Once, I had been taken to see some ghastly waxwork at the Fair, representing I know not what impossible **personage** lying in state. Once, I had been taken to one of our old marsh churches to see a skeleton in the ashes of a rich dress that had been dug out of a vault under the church pavement. Now, waxwork and skeleton seemed to have dark eyes that moved and looked at me. I should have cried out, if I could.

WORD BANK

prominent easily-seen

looking-glass mirror

lustre brightness or brilliance

personage an important or well-known person

Basic reading skills

1 Re-read the first paragraph. List three facts about the room that Pip has entered.

2 In the room, Pip describes 'the strangest lady I have ever seen, or shall ever see'. Summarize what the lady is wearing.

3 Re-read the third paragraph. Select two details that suggest the lady is a wealthy woman.

4 How old do you think the woman in the room is? Refer to evidence in the text to support your answer.

5a Re-read the final paragraph. What two things does Pip compare the lady sitting at the dressing table to?

5b What impression do these comparisons give you of Pip's feelings about the lady? Give reasons for your answer.

6 'I should have cried out, if I could.' What does this sentence suggest about Pip's reaction?

Advanced reading skills

1 Choose one word from the list below that best describes the mood created by this description.

mysterious   sinister   depressing   cheerful   terrifying

Explain your choice of word.

2 Miss Havisham was left at the altar on her wedding day. Read what this student says about the description of Miss Havisham:

The way Miss Havisham is described makes it seem like she is frozen in time.

Can you identify any evidence to support this statement? You could comment on the effects created by the writer's use of:

■ descriptive details

■ comparisons and contrasts

■ vocabulary and sentence forms.

3 How does the way the writer has structured the text help to build a picture of Miss Havisham in the reader's mind? Copy and complete the following table to identify the details the narrator focuses on in each paragraph. Think about whether each paragraph focuses closely on key details or takes a wider look at the character and her surroundings.

Paragraph	Narrator's focus
Paragraph 1	
Paragraph 2	
Paragraph 3	
Paragraph 4	

4   Re-read the following sentence: 'I saw the bride within the bridal dress had withered like the dress, and like the flowers, and had no brightness left but the brightness of her sunken eyes.'

How effective do you find this description? In your answer you should comment on the effects created by:

■ vocabulary choice

■ the comparisons made

■ the details chosen

■ the use of repetition

■ the sentence structure.

Extended reading

Re-read the three extracts in this section and explain which extract provides the most effective description. Refer back to the criteria for an effective description you explored in the 'Before reading' activity on page 122 to support your choice.

Extended writing

Write a description of a familiar place such as a park or playground in a way that creates a tense and unsettling atmosphere. As you write, think about:

- the atmosphere you want to create and how your description of the setting can help to convey this

- how you can use vocabulary and figurative language to create deliberate effects

- the structure of your writing and the way you can guide the reader's eye within and between paragraphs by focusing on particular details or looking at the wider setting.

Remember to check the spelling, punctuation and grammar of your writing.

Early bird

The following sentence is taken from the novel *Jonathan Strange and Mr Norrell* by Susanna Clarke and uses a simile to create a striking description.

'The very shapes of the trees were like frozen screams.'

Select contrasting details from the table below or use your own ideas to create your own striking similes.

swimming pool	dream	book	silence	river
anger	knife	fear	box	kitten
forgotten	thunder	mystery	rage	moonrise
tide	insignificance	fever	kettle	hope
volcano	brave	sunflower	dolphin	imagination

Source texts table

Text	Date
12.1 *The War of the Worlds* by H. G. Wells	1897
12.2 *The Shock of the Fall* by Nathan Filer	2013
12.3 *Hideous Kinky* by Esther Freud	1992

Big picture

How do you feel when you reach the end of a great story? Most authors want to create an ending that has an emotional impact. In a romance story, this might be a feeling of satisfaction that two lovers have been reunited, or in a horror story a sense of dread that stays with the reader long after they have read the final page. In this section, you will read the endings of novels written in the 19th, 20th and 21st centuries and explore the effects these create.

Skills

- Understand the meaning of a text

- Make inferences and refer to evidence in the text

- Explore how a writer's use of language and structure can convey mood, characterization and create a sense of closure

- Use techniques explored in reading, in your own writing

Before reading

1 Look at the following statements about what makes a good ending to a story and rank them in order of importance.

   a All the loose ends of the story should be tied up.

   b The ending of a story should leave you wondering.

   c I think all endings should be happy.

   d The ending should be wrapped up quickly.

   e The ending should show how the characters have changed.

2 Create your own statement about what makes a good ending to a story. You could refer to stories you have read to support your statement.

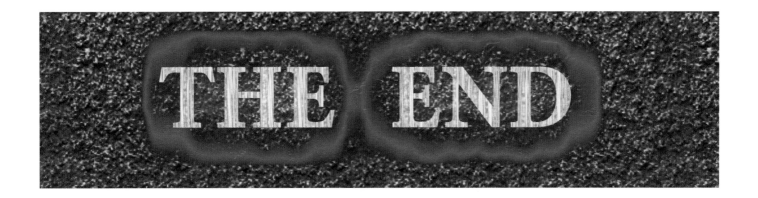

12.1 *The War of the Worlds* by H. G. Wells, 1897

The following extract is the ending of the novel *The War of the Worlds* by H. G. Wells. This novel is about a Martian invasion of Earth which begins when an alien cylinder lands on Horsell Common, near Woking in Surrey. After the Martian fighting machines lay waste to the country, the Martians themselves are eventually killed by the everyday germs that are found on Earth. Here, the narrator reflects on the Martian invasion as life slowly returns to normal. As you read, think about the mood the ending creates.

Source text 12.1

WORD BANK

sidereal with respect to the distant stars (that is, the constellations or fixed stars, not the Sun or planets)

reprieve the cancellation or postponement of a punishment

ordained decided in advance

abiding lasting a long time

artilleryman a soldier who the narrator hid from the Martians

multitudes large numbers of people

phantasms apparitions or ghosts

Before the cylinder fell there was a general persuasion that through all the deep of space no life existed beyond the petty surface of our minute sphere. Now we see further. If the Martians can reach Venus, there is no reason to suppose that the thing is impossible for men, and when the slow cooling of the sun makes this earth uninhabitable, as at last it must do, it may be that the thread of life that has begun here will have streamed out and caught our sister planet within its toils.

Dim and wonderful is the vision I have conjured up in my mind of life spreading slowly from this little seed-bed of the solar system throughout the inanimate vastness of **sidereal** space. But that is a remote dream. It may be, on the other hand, that the destruction of the Martians is only a **reprieve**. To them, and not to us, perhaps, is the future **ordained**.

I must confess the stress and danger of the time have left an **abiding** sense of doubt and insecurity in my mind. I sit in my study writing by lamplight, and suddenly I see again the healing valley below set with writhing flames, and feel the house behind and about me empty and desolate. I go out into the Byfleet Road, and vehicles pass me, a butcher-boy in a cart, a cabful of visitors, a workman on a bicycle, children going to school, and suddenly they become vague and unreal, and I hurry again with the **artilleryman** through the hot, brooding silence. Of a night I see the black powder darkening the silent streets, and the contorted bodies shrouded in that layer; they rise upon me tattered and dog-bitten. They gibber and grow fiercer, paler, uglier, mad distortions of humanity at last, and I wake, cold and wretched, in the darkness of the night.

I go to London and see the busy **multitudes** in Fleet Street and the Strand, and it comes across my mind that they are but the ghosts of the past, haunting the streets that I have seen silent and wretched, going to and fro, **phantasms** in a dead city, the mockery of life in a

WORD BANK

galvanized shocked or
    excited into action

tumult loud, confused
    noise

galvanized body. And strange, too, it is to stand on Primrose Hill, as I did but a day before writing this last chapter, to see the great province of houses, dim and blue through the haze of the smoke and mist, vanishing at last into the vague lower sky, to see the people walking to and fro among the flower-beds on the hill, to see the sightseers about the Martian machine that stands there still, to hear the **tumult** of playing children, and to recall the time when I saw it all bright and clear-cut, hard and silent, under the dawn of that last great day...

And strangest of all is it to hold my wife's hand again, and to think that I have counted her, and that she has counted me, among the dead.

Basic reading skills

1   'Before the cylinder fell there was a general persuasion that through all the deep of space no life existed beyond the petty surface of our minute sphere.'

    Explain what people generally believed before 'the cylinder fell'.

2   Re-read the opening paragraph.

    a Why does the narrator suggest the Earth will eventually become uninhabitable?

    b What does the narrator suggest the human race will do when the Earth becomes uninhabitable?

3   Re-read the paragraph beginning 'Dim and wonderful is the vision...' Pick out the quotation that suggests the narrator is worried that the Martians might return.

4   List three details that show the narrator is still affected by the 'stress and danger' of the Martian invasion.

5   'And strangest of all is it to hold my wife's hand again, and to think that I have counted her, and that she has counted me, among the dead.'

    Explain what this sentence means in your own words.

Advanced reading skills

1a What mood does the ending of this novel create? Pick a word from the list below or choose your own.

optimistic

pessimistic

bleak

hopeful

uncertain

1b Select a quotation that you think is particularly effective in helping to create this mood. Explain your choice.

2 Re-read the paragraph beginning 'Dim and wonderful is the vision...'

   a What two alternative futures for the human race does the writer contrast here?

   b Which do you think the narrator believes is the more likely future? Support your answer with evidence from the text.

3 Re-read the lines below and explore the effects created by the writer's use of language. You should comment on:

- the writer's choice of verbs and adjectives

- the sentence forms and the effects these create.

'Of a night I see the black powder darkening the silent streets, and the contorted bodies shrouded in that layer; they rise upon me tattered and dog-bitten. They gibber and grow fiercer, paler, uglier, mad distortions of humanity at last, and I wake, cold and wretched, in the darkness of the night.'

4 Look at the following statement from a student about the ending:

The shift in focus from looking at the universe at the beginning to the narrator holding his wife's hand at the end emphasizes how small and vulnerable the human race is.

Do you agree or disagree with this statement? Find evidence from the text to support your point of view.

12.2 *The Shock of the Fall* by Nathan Filer, 2013

The following extract is the ending of the novel *The Shock of the Fall* by Nathan Filer. This novel is about a 19-year-old man named Matt who suffers from mental illness. When staying in hospital, Matt writes down his thoughts and feelings using an old typewriter, especially about his older brother Simon, who died when they were both children. Here, after a memorial service Matt has organized to remember his brother, he reflects on what the end of the story is.

Source text 12.2

WORD BANK

Hope Road Day Centre a day centre for mental health patients which is being closed down

keepsake a small item kept in memory of the person who gave it or originally owned it

This story doesn't have an end. Not really. How can it when I'm still here, still living it? When I print out these last pages I'll turn the computer off, and later today men will come with boxes to take everything away. The lights of **Hope Road Day Centre** will be switched off for the last time. But in time, another day centre will open and close, and another, and there will always be a Nurse This and a Nurse That, a *Click-Click-Wink* and a Claire-or-maybe-Anna.

I've told you about my first stretch in hospital, but I've been back in since. And I know I will again. We move in circles, this illness and me. We are electrons orbiting a nucleus.

The plan is always the same: After I'm discharged, I spend a couple of weeks with my parents to help me to settle. Mum wishes I was nine again; we could build a den in the living room, and hide away forever. Dad takes it seriously. He holds back on the special handshakes and talks to me like I'm a man. They're both helpful in their own way. The first few days are hardest. The silence is a problem. I get used to the hourly checks, the scraping of viewing slats, fragments of conversations drifting from the nurses' office. I get used to having Simon around. It takes time to adjust, and time to adjust when he's gone.

I could keep on going, but you know what I'm like. The ink running dry from my typewriter ribbon. This place shutting down. That's enough small print to get anyone thinking.

So I'll stack these pages with the rest of them, and leave it all behind. Writing about the past is a way of reliving it, a way of seeing it unfold all over again. We place memories on pieces of paper to know they will always exist. But this story has never been a **keepsake** – it's finding a way to let go. I don't know the ending, but I know what happens next. I walk along the corridor towards the sound of a Goodbye Party. But I won't get that far. I'll take a left, then a right, and I will push open the front door with both hands.

I have nothing else to do today.

It's a beginning.

Basic reading skills

1 Re-read the first paragraph. Explain in your own words why the narrator says, 'This story doesn't have an end.'

2 Summarize how the narrator's mother and father treat him differently.

3 List two sources of noise the narrator gets used to when he stays in hospital.

4 What two reasons does the narrator give for stopping writing his story?

5 Where does the writer go at the end of the extract?

Advanced reading skills

1 Re-read the following lines and explain what the writer's choice of metaphor suggests about the narrator's mental illness: 'We move in circles, this illness and me. We are electrons orbiting a nucleus.'

2 Re-read the paragraph beginning 'The plan is always the same...' Explain what impression you get of the narrator's parents.

3 Re-read the paragraph beginning 'So I'll stack these pages with the rest of them...'

   a Why does the narrator suggest that people write about the past?

   b What reason does the narrator give for writing his story?

4 How does the writer's use of language and sentence forms help to convey an impression of the narrator and his thoughts and feelings? In your answer you should comment on:

   ■ the conversational tone of the writing

   ■ the use of the present tense

   ■ the use of repetition

   ■ how other language features and sentence forms contribute to the impression given.

5 Choose the following statement that you most agree with and finish it off in your own words. Refer to details in the text to support your statement.

   I think the ending is an optimistic one because...

   I think the ending is a pessimistic one because...

12.3 *Hideous Kinky* by Esther Freud, 1992

The following extract is taken from the novel *Hideous Kinky* by Esther Freud. Set in Morocco during the 1960s, the novel is about a young girl called Lucy and her older sister Bea, who are taken from London to Marrakech, a city in Morocco, by their mother Julia. There, Julia meets a Moroccan man named Bilal who becomes almost like a father to Lucy and Bea. Here at the end of the novel, Julia has decided to take Lucy and Bea back home to London, and Bilal is taking them all to the train station through the streets of Marrakech. However, it is the King of Morocco's birthday, so the streets are very crowded.

Source text 12.3

WORD BANK

Mary, Mary-Rose and Rosemary hand-sewn dolls that Lucy and Bea try to sell

Berber the indigenous people of North Africa

Red Indian old-fashioned term for American Indian, now seen as dated and offensive

A crack like thunder shook the air. The street where we stood cleared as if by magic and the people pressed themselves back against the buildings and craned their necks to see. Bilal lifted me on to his shoulders. A group of men with guns marched into view. They were followed by an army of horses that trotted and scampered, their tails arched and their heads held high. Their riders wore swords that curved down from their belts, and their clothes were trimmed with braid. I could feel the hearts of a thousand people stopping and starting. And then an open carriage rolled into view. It was drawn by four black horses. Inside sat the King of Morocco. The voice of the crowd burst out in a frenzy of delight. They shouted and strained and waved their arms at him, and in return the King stood up in his carriage and put his hand over his heart.

We streamed after the King's carriage. We were squeezed through the gate of the city and emerged on the plain where once we had tried to sell **Mary, Mary-Rose and Rosemary**. As the King's carriage rolled through the gates, a line of **Berber** horsemen, who had been waiting in a silent salute, raised their guns and at sudden speed charged the carriage. The city froze as the horses thundered down on the King. Until with a simultaneous ringing shot of their rifles they skidded to a halt. I watched spellbound from Bilal's shoulders. The men charged and the Berber women danced. They accompanied themselves with a noise like a **Red Indian** whoop that made me laugh. It ended on a short shriek like a marsh bird.

'We've missed our train, surely,' Mum called, and we began to extricate ourselves from the crowd, to squeeze and shoulder our way back through the hustle of the celebrations to find a taxi that was not on holiday.

Our train was waiting. Bilal got on with us and found a place where we could sit beside a window. He packed our bags into the racks above the seat. I was wrong. He is coming with us, I thought, and as I thought it, Bilal was walking backwards, smiling with his smiling eyes until, without a word, he had disappeared among the last-minute passengers. Bea and I searched the length of the train and hung out of every window, willing him to reappear.

'Bilal! Bilal!' we shouted as the train began to pull away. 'Bilal!' But I couldn't pick him out among the crowd dispersing on the platform.

The train rumbled down a track banked with the first flowers of spring, with wild hollyhocks and tiny clinging roses, and entered the gloom of an avenue of eucalyptus trees. Marrakech stretched behind us in the distance.

'Does this train go all the way home?' I asked Mum, who was braiding and unbraiding her hair with quick, distracted fingers.

'No,' she said. I had to pinch her for the answer.

Bea had climbed up into an empty luggage rack and was using it as a hammock. 'Hideous, hideous, hideous kinky, hideous, hideous kink,' she chanted softly to the rhythm of the wheels.

I badly wanted to climb up and join her, but I thought it would be safest to stay on the seat in case Mum changed her mind about going home and decided at the last minute to jump off at one of the stations along the way.

Basic reading skills

1 Re-read the first paragraph.

a Rearrange the following into the order the narrator sees them, from first to last:

An open carriage drawn by four black horses

A group of young men with guns

An army of horses

The King of Morocco standing up

b How does Lucy get a good view of the events of this paragraph?

2 Re-read the second paragraph. Pick out a quotation that suggests Lucy is impressed by the spectacle described.

3a Pick out the quotation that you think best shows Lucy's feelings towards Bilal.

3b Explain what your chosen quotation suggests about Lucy's feelings towards Bilal.

4 Lucy asks her mum if the train they are on goes all the way home. How does she get her to answer this question?

5 Why does Lucy decide to stay on her seat on the train rather than climbing up to join Bea in the luggage rack?

Advanced reading skills

1 Which word would you choose to describe the mood of this ending? Give reasons for your choice.

hopeful

sad

joyful

bittersweet

depressing

2 Why do you think the writer has chosen to juxtapose the King's procession with Lucy and her family's departure from Marrakech? What effect does this contrast create?

3 Read the following statement by a student about the ending:

Stories are about a character's journey, so it feels right to end this story with Lucy heading home.

Do you agree or disagree with this statement? Explain your answer with reference to the text.

4 Re-read the final paragraph, which consists of a single sentence. What does this paragraph suggest about the relationship between Lucy and her mother?

In your answer you should comment on:

- what this sentence suggests about Lucy's character

- what this sentence suggests about Lucy's mother

- the impression this gives you about their relationship.

Re-read the three extracts in this section and explain which you think is the best ending. Refer back to the criteria for a good ending you explored in the 'Before reading' activity on page 133 to support your choice.

Extended writing

Write the ending of a story where the protagonist is returning home after a long and difficult journey. You could use the following lines to begin your ending:

> I looked up and saw my home in the distance, a single light glowing in the window. As the storm raged around me, I stumbled forward...

As you write, think about:

- who the protagonist is and where they have been

- what the protagonist's emotions might be and how they might share these

- who might be waiting and how they will react when the protagonist returns

- the atmosphere you want to create and how you can use description, action and dialogue to help to convey this

- how you can use vocabulary and figurative language to create deliberate effects

- the structure of your writing and the way you can guide the reader's eye within and between paragraphs

- the emotion you want the reader to feel at the end of this story and how your final line can help to evoke this emotion.

Remember to check the spelling, punctuation and grammar of your writing.

Early bird

How many different ways can you write the following sentence?

> *He was soon borne away by the waves and lost in darkness and distance.*

You can reorder, expand or omit details, changing punctuation if required, but you must keep the meaning of the sentence the same. Then choose the version of the sentence you think would make the most effective ending for a story.

Glossary

adjective
a word that describes a noun

adverb
a word that adds to the meaning of a verb, adjective or another adverb

adverbial
of time a word or phrase that is used as an adverb to indicate when something happened, for how long or the frequency of an action

cliché
an idea that is used so often that it has little meaning

conjunction
a word that usually joins words, phrases or clauses in a sentence, for example, *and, but, although*

connotation
an idea or meaning suggested by a word or phrase

contrast
a difference clearly seen when things are compared or seen together

extended metaphor
a metaphor which is continued through a series of lines or sentences in a text

figurative language
language that uses words for the effects they create, rather than their literal meanings

foreshadowing
a literary technique where words and phrases are used to hint about what is going to happen in the story

formality
how formal or informal the language used is as indicated by vocabulary choice, sentence forms, use of Standard English and so on

genre
a particular style or type of story

hyperbole
a deliberately exaggerated statement that is not meant to be taken literally

imagery
writing which creates a picture or appeals to other senses – this includes simile, metaphor and personification and the use of vivid verbs, nouns, adjectives and adverbs

melodramatic
characteristic of melodrama, especially in being exaggerated or over-emotional

metaphor
the use of a word or phrase which describes something by likening it to something else

motif
an image that is repeated in a literary work

narrative viewpoint
the perspective a story is told from, for example, first person

narrative voice
the voice that tells the story

narrator
the person or character who recounts the events of a story

non-standard personal pronouns
not of the form that is accepted as standard, that is, 'me uncle' instead of 'my uncle'

onomatopoeia
words which imitate the sounds they represent

pathetic fallacy
a literary technique where a character's emotions are reflected or represented by the environment or landscape

preposition
a word used with a noun or pronoun to show place, position, time or means, for example, *over* the roadway

protagonist
the main character

repetition
words or phrases which are repeated for effect

sentence forms
sentence types (that is, statement, question, command, exclamation) and sentence structures (that is, single and multiclause sentences)

setting
the time and place in which a story is set

simile
a comparison where one thing is compared to another using the words like or as

symbol
something representing or standing for something else (often a physical thing representing something non-physical)

theme
an idea that emerges from a literary work's treatment of its subject-matter or a topic that recurs in it

tone
a manner of expression in speech or writing

verb
a word that identifies actions, thoughts, feelings or the state of being